Zora Neale Hurston's Final Decade

UNIVERSITY PRESS OF FLORIDA

Florida A&M University, Tallahassee
Florida Atlantic University, Boca Raton
Florida Gulf Coast University, Ft. Myers
Florida International University, Miami
Florida State University, Tallahassee
New College of Florida, Sarasota
University of Central Florida, Orlando
University of Florida, Gainesville
University of North Florida, Jacksonville
University of South Florida, Tampa
University of West Florida, Pensacola

ZORA NEALE HURSTON'S FINAL DECADE

Virginia Lynn Moylan

❖ ❖ ❖

UNIVERSITY PRESS OF FLORIDA

Gainesville · Tallahassee · Tampa · Boca Raton
Pensacola · Orlando · Miami · Jacksonville · Ft. Myers · Sarasota

Copyright 2011 by Virginia Lynn Moylan
Printed in the United States of America. This book is printed on Glatfelter
Natures Book, a paper certified under the standards of the Forestry Steward-
ship Council (FSC). It is a recycled stock that contains 30 percent post-
consumer waste and is acid-free.

16 15 14 13 12 11   6 5 4 3 2 1

Library of Congress Cataloging-in-Publication Data
Moylan, Virginia Lynn.
Zora Neale Hurston's final decade / Virginia Lynn Moylan.
p. cm.
Includes bibliographical references and index.
ISBN 978-0-8130-3578-9 (alk. paper)
1. Hurston, Zora Neale—Last years. 2. Hurston, Zora Neale—Homes and
haunts—Florida. 3. Authors, American—Homes and haunts—Florida.
4. Authors, American—20th century—Biography. 5. African American women
authors—Biography. 6. African American authors—Biography. I. Title.
PS3515.U789Z788 2011
813.'52—dc22
[B]
2010040994

The University Press of Florida is the scholarly publishing agency for the State
University System of Florida, comprising Florida A&M University, Florida
Atlantic University, Florida Gulf Coast University, Florida International Uni-
versity, Florida State University, New College of Florida, University of Central
Florida, University of Florida, University of North Florida, University of South
Florida, and University of West Florida.

University Press of Florida
15 Northwest 15th Street
Gainesville, FL 32611-2079
http://www.upf.com

In memory of my beloved mother Virginia Poppell
and my mentor Sara Lee Creech
and to my precious children Kathleen and William Fallon

CONTENTS

Zora Neale Hurston's Final Decade

INTRODUCTION

Alice Walker once declared that "no one could wish for a more advantageous heritage than that bequeathed to the black writer in the South."[1] A stronger case for a black southern writer who took advantage of this blessing could not be made than for that of writer, folklorist, and anthropologist Zora Neale Hurston, who framed the lives of southern black folk with all of their juices, drama, creativity, wit, and humor intact. Her intimate knowledge of religion, black southern folklore, and verbal art imbued her writings with a spice and humor that set her apart from her contemporaries and inspired Walker to proclaim her a "Genius of the South" (a tribute that she had engraved on Hurston's tombstone). Her determination to faithfully chronicle the culturally rich lives of working- and lower-class blacks, whom she referred to as the "the Negro farthest down," has given us a treasure trove of early twentieth-century black southern folklore that would have otherwise been lost.

My fascination with Hurston and her work began in 1992, when I experienced a kind of "baptism by fire" as a beginning teacher in Pahokee—a small, impoverished city on the banks of Lake Okeechobee at the northern tip of the Florida Glades. Faced with a population of predominately poor black students suffering from low self-esteem and academic failure, I decided that the standard methods of teaching, which had failed them year after year, would simply not do. With that failure in mind, I decided to teach writing with a generous helping of life lessons through the production of a cultural magazine titled

Grassy Waters ("Pa-hay-ho-kee" means grassy waters in Seminole Indian). The magazine, we decided, would feature engaging articles about the colorful people, culture, and history of the Glades.

While researching ideas for the first issue, I came across an extraordinary white former Belle Glade resident, Sara Lee Creech. Having seen the need to offer an affordable and culturally acceptable alternative to the insulting caricatures that passed for black dolls, Ms. Creech had in 1951 conceived and produced the first "anthropologically correct" (Hurston coined the phrase) quality black baby doll to be manufactured and sold in America.

Thrilled that we had come across the originator of what was surely one of the most significant cultural advances in race relations since the Civil War, my students and I invited Ms. Creech (who had since moved forty-five miles west to Lake Worth) to our school to be interviewed. The result of her generous acceptance would ultimately inspire me and my students far beyond expectations and mark the beginning of my glorious obsession with all things Hurston and the writing of this book.

A seasoned raconteur in her own right, Ms. Creech, we soon discovered, had enjoyed a deep, enduring friendship with Hurston and had persuaded her to move to Belle Glade in the early 1950s. Over the course of an hour, my students and I enjoyed a rare first-hand account of Hurston's tenacity, spirit, and courage. We learned of her struggles and triumphs as a black female writer at a time when few black females wrote books and few blacks bought them and when peonage, segregation, and racial violence were a way of life in the South.

Creech described Zora as a strong, attractive, bodacious, woman who lived her life on her own terms, refusing to be limited by racism or sexism. She was a generous and supportive friend who, along with first lady Eleanor Roosevelt, helped Creech in her efforts to create and promote her lovely and culturally sensitive Saralee doll.

In the months that followed, having developed a keen interest in Hurston's work and life, my students and I avidly read her autobiography *Dust Tracks on a Road* and her most popular novel, *Their Eyes Were Watching God*. And having been both impressed and inspired by

Ms. Creech, I continued to visit her at her home in Lake Worth, spending countless hours engaged in sometimes deep, always memorable, and more often than not humorous conversations about life and Zora. (Sadly, Ms. Creech passed away at age 92 in 2008.)

One of the insights I gleaned from our conversations was the lack of detailed information surrounding the last decade of Hurston's life—a period that has often been dismissed as "a career in ruins" or "a terrible decade." Robert Hemenway's remarkable *Zora Neale Hurston: A Literary Biography* (1977) offered the first critical look at what was known of her oeuvre in the context of her life and times but included scant details surrounding Hurston's last ten years, a decade that was preceded by a sex scandal in which she was falsely accused of molesting three adolescent boys. The morals charges, which were brought against her in Harlem in 1948, created a scandal that many believe destroyed her reputation and her career. The most recent biography, *Wrapped in Rainbows* (2003), by Valerie Boyd, is the most complete biography thus far. However, as richly detailed as it is, it does not include many of the available facts, interviews, research, or close examination of the political and social milieu that greatly influenced Hurston's life and work during the 1950s that is offered here. While I commend both biographers for their diligent research and remarkable contributions to our understanding of Hurston and her work, I also submit that no biographer can be expected to ferret out every detail or consider every facet of a person's life. Although we now know more about Hurston than ever, there are still facts to be uncovered and questions to be answered.

In addition to the excellent Boyd and Hemenway biographies and Alice Walker and Mary Helen Washington's *I Love Myself When I'm Laughing . . . and Then Again When I'm Looking Mean and Impressive*, Hurston's life and accomplishments have been further illuminated by Carla Kaplan's *Zora Neale Hurston: A Life in Letters* and Deborah Plant's *Zora Neale Hurston: A Biography of the Spirit* and *Every Tub Must Sit on Its Own Bottom: The Philosophy and Politics of Zora Neale Hurston*. Other notable contributions include Tiffany Ruby Patterson's *Zora Neale Hurston: A Study of Southern Life*, John Lowe's *Jump at the Sun: Zora Neale Hurston's Cosmic Comedy*, Lynda Marion Hill's *Social Rituals and the Verbal Art of Zora Neale Hurston*, and Pamela Bordelon's *Go Gator and Muddy the Water: Writing by Zora Neale Hurston from the Federal Writers' Project*.

In 2005, Oprah Winfrey's lush television production of Hurston's *Their Eyes Were Watching God*, starring Halle Berry, brought the classic love story to life for millions of fans. Kristy Anderson's discovery of a collection of Hurston's Negro folktales from the Gulf states and her biographical documentary *Zora Neale Hurston: Jump at the Sun*, which aired on PBS in the spring of 2008, have also made significant contributions to the Hurston canon. Jose Garofalo has also produced *That's Livin': The Zora Neale Hurston Story*, an excellent docudrama that chronicles Hurston's life.

The aim of this book is to add another layer of facts to what is already known about Hurston's final years and to provide a fresh interpretation and assessment of her controversial social and political views and writings during the racially and politically charged 1950s.

The biographical sketch that begins this book provides an overview of the highlights of Hurston's life through 1948 and serves as a frame of reference for some of the events and people mentioned in the later chapters. Included are new details about the members of the Hurston family who settled in Sanford in the late 1800s; an interview with Elizabeth Howard, who visited Zora when she lived on the *Wanago* in Daytona Beach; and an account of one of Hurston's folklore-collecting expeditions in a turpentine camp in White Springs. Additional details about the year Hurston lived with her brother John and his wife Blanche in Jacksonville in 1914 and a valuable excerpt from a previously unpublished letter from Hurston to her estranged husband Albert Price are also featured.

Chapter 1, "In Hell's Basement," begins in 1948 in Harlem with the retelling of Hurston's spirit-crushing ordeal following the false molestation charges brought against her by her former Harlem landlady and her son. The scandal, which almost drove her to suicide, was sensationalized by a black newspaper that ignored the facts in order to maximize its profits. It also includes details about a personal vendetta by Richard Rochester to further destroy Hurston's reputation for the purpose of revenge.

Chapter 2, "Sunshine and Southern Politics," begins with Hurston's return to Florida in 1950. This chapter examines her social and political philosophies and her controversial response to the highly volatile climate in the South brought about by the Cold War, President Truman's civil rights proposals, and the 1944 Supreme Court's ruling in *Smith v. Albright*, which gave blacks the right to vote in the South's historically all-white primaries. It also explores Hurston's relationship with Congressman George W. Smathers and his family and her support for his U.S. Senate campaign against incumbent Claude Pepper in the Florida Democratic primary.

Chapter 3, "Sara Creech and Her Beautiful Doll," sheds new light on the six months she lived in Belle Glade in 1951 and includes details about her friendship with Sara Lee and Mary Creech, her involvement in and support for the work of the Belle Glade Inter-Racial Council, and the vital role she played in the production and promotion of Saralee, the nation's first quality, affordable black baby doll. This chapter also highlights the race and gender issues Hurston confronted in her determination to challenge the literary, social, and cultural status quo.

Chapter 4, "Herod the Sun-Like Splendor," follows Hurston from Belle Glade to her beloved Eau Gallie home and draws upon interviews with her friends and former neighbors. The chapter focuses on Hurston's passionate obsession with King Herod, the ruler of Judea from 40 B.C.E. to 4 B.C.E. and the subject of her last manuscript. The myths and realities of Herod's life, leadership, and spectacular career are explored through an examination of Hurston's research and through her "Herod the Great" manuscript, which challenges the biblical depiction of Herod as a tyrannical killer of infants and the biased account of Herod written by first-century Jewish historian Flavius Josephus.

Chapter 5, "Death on the Suwannee," is a detailed account of Hurston's involvement in and coverage of the sensational murder trial of Ruby McCollum, a wealthy black woman who murdered her white lover, Leroy Adams, a popular physician and newly elected Florida state legislator. In 1952, Hurston agreed to travel to Live Oak, a bastion of the Ku Klux Klan, to cover the trial for the *Pittsburgh Courier*, the nation's most popular black weekly newspaper. Appalled by the judge's refusal to grant Ruby her civil rights and the kangaroo court atmosphere, Hurston called upon her friend, journalist and civil rights advocate William Bradford Huie, to intervene.

Chapter 6, "A Crisis in Dixie," provides historical context for Hurston's highly controversial opposition to the Supreme Court's 1954 ruling in *Brown v. Board of Education* and examines the validity of some of her objections. Taking a fresh look at Hurston's position, this chapter relies on recent studies and personal accounts that document the consequences black students and their communities suffered under the provisions of *Brown*, which, in retrospect, serve to justify some of Hurston's most contentious views.

Chapter 7, "The Last Horizon," provides an in-depth description of the last few years of Hurston's life in Fort Pierce, where she briefly worked as a reporter for the *Fort Pierce Chronicle* and as an English teacher at Lincoln Park Academy. This chapter relies on interviews with many of her friends as well as her former Lincoln Park Academy students and colleagues and includes a detailed account of her funeral.

ZORA NEALE HURSTON

A Biographical Sketch, 1891–1948

*I have memories within that came out of the material that went
in to make me. Time and place have had their say. So you will
have to know something about the time and place where I came
from, in order that you may interpret the incidents and directions
of my life.*

Given Zora Neale Hurston's inextricable ties to the state of Florida,
it was only fitting that she would spend her final decade on its sandy
shores. Known as the Sunshine State, Florida has been a mecca for the
rich, a refuge for the lawless, a haven for the retired, and many other
things to its countless residents and tourists. To Hurston, Florida was
the principal highway of her imagination, a richly textured mosaic of
southern black folk culture that both fueled and enriched her art.

She was born in Notasulga, Alabama, on January 7, 1891, but never
publicly acknowledged it. In her autobiography, *Dust Tracks on a Road*
(1942), she moved her birth date a decade forward and declared Eatonville, Florida, one of the nation's first self-governed, all-black towns,
as her birthplace, home village, and greatest source of inspiration.
By all accounts, it was in this tiny hamlet, where the folks were as
colorful as the foliage, that Hurston developed a lifelong passion for
storytelling.

Her parents, John Cornelius Hurston and Lucy Ann Potts, were
native Alabamians. John came from a family of poor sharecroppers,
and Lucy's parents were prosperous landowners who bitterly opposed
their union. After their marriage in 1882, the couple moved into a

small cabin on a cotton plantation, owned by a white man believed to have been John's biological father, where John made his living as a plantation foreman and carpenter.[1] Eleven years and six children later, John abandoned the economic limitations of plantation life and headed for the booming citrus belt of Central Florida, where he quickly established himself in the fledgling town of Eatonville.

Situated on the edge of Florida's raw frontier, Eatonville was an African American paradise. The establishment of the all-black township near the turn of the century was nothing short of a miracle in the racist South. In *Dust Tracks*, Hurston compared it to "hitting a straight lick with a crooked stick."[2] After the Civil War, large plantations were divided into small parcels that were sold more often to poor whites than to the few African Americans who had the capital to buy. When Reconstruction ended in 1877 and white southern leadership returned to power, local judges were known to convict innocent blacks of vagrancy and sentence them to the chain gang simply for demanding to vote or trying to homestead their own land.[3]

By the time of Eatonville's founding in 1887, the abolishment of the Civil Rights Act of 1875, the enactment of Jim Crow laws, and the establishment of a poll tax had systematically stripped African Americans of any chance for social and political equality or economic prosperity. But Eatonville, where the Hurstons were freed from the chains of white oppression, profoundly changed the destiny of the family and served as a powerful symbol of racial pride and the spirit of possibilities.

As a skilled carpenter, John Hurston was assured a good living, but his spellbinding oratory became his stock in trade. Soon after moving to Eatonville, he was called to the pulpit of the Zion Baptist Church in the neighboring community of Sanford, where he became well known for his "colorful sermons and forceful delivery."[4] With the support of a growing congregation, John eventually purchased five acres of Eatonville property that included guava trees and an orange grove, built his family an eight-room residence with a meat house and a barn, and later purchased a home in Sanford.

Eatonville society revolved around three institutions: the family, the church, and the Hungerford Industrial and Normal School. Established by Russell and Mary Calhoun in 1889, Hungerford, the first and only school for black children in the area, was a model of excellence: "Inspiration, motivation, and the development of a positive self image were the driving forces of all students who attended the school. The insistence on excellence was paramount. . . . Students were taught to set goals and to work toward the achievement of those goals with dignity and respect."[5]

Hungerford's educational philosophies, which reflected the beliefs and work ethics of Tuskegee Institute founder Booker T. Washington, had a profound influence on the development of the community as well as on Zora's social and political views. The bedrock of Washington's beliefs was that all obstacles, including racism, could be overcome through the power of individual merit. He believed that hard work and accomplishment were the keys to self-empowerment, self-sufficiency, and racial equality: "I have found that . . . it is the visible, the tangible that softens racial prejudice. The actual sight of a first-class house that a Negro has built is ten times more potent than pages of discussion about a house that he ought to build, or perhaps could build."[6]

This philosophy, which epitomized the ideals of Eatonville's founders, remained the guiding force behind Zora's fierce individualism, which she refused to abandon under any circumstances. It also formed the basis for the development of many of her controversial political and social philosophies later in life.

Eatonville and the folks who lived there have garnered legendary status as the setting and characters for much of Hurston's fiction. Her fondest and most vivid childhood memories centered on her home village, where the simplest townsfolk were endowed with a gift for fanciful simile and extravagant metaphorical expression. For instance, a person of uncommon intelligence or talent was described as "a whirlwind among breezes." Their characteristically colorful language resulted, as one writer explains it, "when African people with an intensely musical and oral culture came up hard against the King James Bible and the sweet talking South."[7] This idiom, wrapped in image and sound, was showcased in Hurston's fiction and formed the basis for what biographer Robert Hemenway called her "evangelical zeal for the form and substance of black folk art."[8]

Hurston's favorite place in town was the front porch of Joe Clarke's general store, the hub of the town's social life, where the master storytellers spun their tales and the adult gossip often included "sly references to the physical condition of women, irregular love affairs, or male potency."[9] Children were banned from hanging around the porch too long, but Zora would risk a whipping to hide around the side and listen to the tales, the gossip, a singing liner's work song, or the soulful melodies of Bubber Mimms's guitar. She was mesmerized by the menfolk's "lying sessions"—otherwise known as folktales—about creation, servitude, love, death, nature, and the why of things, tales in which "God, Devil, Brer Rabbit, Brer Fox, Sis Cat, Brer Bear, Brer Lion, Tiger, Buzzard, and all the wood folk walked and talked like natural men."[10]

In later years, Hurston captured on paper some of the humorous one-upmanship of Eatonville's porch dwellers, which she contributed to the Florida Writers' Project folklore collection of the 1930s:

Teller one: "Oh, I seen a man so ugly that he could set up behind a jimson weed and hatch monkeys."

Teller two: "Oh, that man wasn't ugly! I knowed a man that could set up behind a tombstone and hatch hants."

Teller Three: "Aw, them wasn't so ugly men you all is talking about! Fact is, them is pretty mens. I knowed a man and he was so ugly that you throw him in the Mississippi River and skim ugly for six months."

When they'd exhausted one subject, they'd move on to the next:

Teller Four: "They have strong winds on the Florida west coast, too. One day the wind blowed so hard till it blowed a well out of the ground. Then one day it blowed so hard till it blowed a crooked road straight. Another time it blowed and blowed and scattered the days of the week so bad till Sunday didn't come until late Tuesday evening."[11]

As Zora tells it, in her youth she was an imaginative, headstrong, rough-and-tumble tomboy with a passionate wanderlust. She loved to read and tell her own folktales and was undeniably "Mama's child." Lucy Hurston, for whom she framed her warmest memories, fostered her daughter's self-confidence and encouraged her creativity. In her autobiography, Hurston described her mother, a former school-teacher, as an extraordinary woman who possessed not only the confidence and intelligence to advise her husband in his church and business affairs but also the backbone to deal with his philandering. She was a devoted mother who taught her two daughters and five sons the rudiments of reading, writing, and arithmetic before they were old enough for school and encouraged them to "jump at de sun."

John Hurston, whom Zora characterized as "two hundred pounds of bone and muscle," could build a house, farm the land, and preach the water right out of the ocean. In addition to his churches (in Sanford and later in Oviedo), he served as pastor of Eatonville's Macedonia Baptist Church for fifteen years and moderator of the South Florida Missionary Baptist Association from 1900 to 1902. He also served as Eatonville's third mayor from 1912 to 1916, writing many of its municipal codes.

Zora was mesmerized by the thunder-and-lightening poetry in her father's sermons and used him as a model for characters in her stories and novels (her parents were most notably featured in her first novel, *Jonah's Gourd Vine*, published in 1934). And when groups of ministers gathered at her father's house for regular meetings, she was captivated by their big storytelling sessions, which she amusingly recounted in *Dust Tracks*.

There is little doubt that Hurston admired her father, but their personal relationship was famously strained. While Lucy Hurston encouraged her daughter's confidence, her father viewed her head-strong ways as impertinence that would get her hung by white folks and shunned Zora in favor of her older sister, Sarah. She coped with his rejection by convincing herself that his approval was neither needed nor wanted.

Zora claimed to have had prophetic visions that began at age seven. The first of these visions, in which she saw her family broken and herself orphaned, friendless, and wandering, became a reality on September 18, 1904, when her beloved mother died of what was likely pneumonia. About that tragedy Zora wrote: "Death stirred from his platform in his secret place in our yard, and came inside the house.... Mama died at sundown and changed a world. That is a world which had been built out of her body and her heart."[12]

The death of her mother marked the beginning of one of the darkest and most painful periods of Hurston's life. In the blink of an eye, a life that had been filled with love and stability changed to estrangement and uncertainty. Her father's indifference and the loss of her protector, nurturer, and central driving force just as she was entering adolescence left Zora emotionally rudderless and bereft. Shortly after her mother's funeral, she was brusquely shuffled off to Florida Baptist Academy, a private boarding school in Jacksonville, along with two of her older siblings, Sara and Robert. It might have been some comfort having her older sister for support, but Sara returned home after only a few weeks.

Five months later, her father shocked the family by marrying 20-year-old Mattie Mogue, a member of his Oviedo church congregation. Mattie was half John Hurston's age and, according to Zora, spiteful, jealous, self-serving, and unwilling to care for her husband's younger children. Confrontations with her new stepmother, whom Zora later referred to as "The Black Anne Boleyn," eventually drove Zora's sister Sara into an early marriage. In addition, for unexplained reasons, John Hurston stopped paying Zora's tuition, forcing her to earn her own way.

When the school year ended, she returned to her father's house with disastrous consequences. The extreme animosity Zora felt toward

Mattie resulted in a violent confrontation between them and created a chasm between Zora and her father that lasted until his death in Memphis in 1918.

The next six years of Hurston's life, from ages fourteen to nineteen, were haunted, miserable, and lonely. She had lost her mother to death, her father to indifference, and her home to Mattie: "I could not bear the air for miles around. It was too personal and pressing and humid with memories of what used to be."[13] Unable to live in her father's house, she eventually sought refuge with friends and family. But she found comfort and peace nowhere. She drifted from one house to another, from Eatonville to Maitland and Sanford, attending school sporadically and cleaning white folks' homes to earn her keep.

In her autobiography, Hurston is purposely vague about her whereabouts during this time. However, she did claim to have briefly lived in Sanford with her brother Dick and his new wife. Given her longing for family closeness and her hopes of going back to school, it is likely that she spent more of what has been referred to as those "lost years" in Sanford than she revealed. There she would have had the opportunity to live with or close to a cluster of other family members, including her uncles Isaiah Hurston and James Potts, who had followed her parents to Florida and settled in Sanford's black Georgetown community.[14]

According to the Orange County Black Communities Survey, James (Jim) Potts, Lucy Hurston's brother, moved to Sanford in 1895 and used his family wealth to acquire extensive land holdings. After marrying Dolly Watts in Orange County on September 12, 1898, the couple purchased and operated a grocery store next to their home at 518 East 8th Street. Their daughter Mary grew up and married Mack C. Mosely, a relative of Eatonville's Mosely family, for whom Zora had great affection.[15] Sanford was also the location of her father's second home on the corner of Hickory and 6th streets.[16]

A skilled carpenter and a deacon of John Hurston's Sanford church, Isaiah Hurston lived with his family on 8th Street in the same modest house where Zora, who remained close to her uncle's family all her life, completed *Jonah's Gourd Vine*.[17]

Zora's early presence in Sanford is also documented by a small but significant entry in an official survey of Orange County black communities. The survey, which contains short biographical information on Georgetown residents, includes a paragraph on Zora taken from the *American Guide* written by Margaret Barnes in 1936: "Zora Neale Hurston is our [Sanford's] main claim to distinction among our colored race. She was born in Eatonville . . . and came to Sanford at a young age and lived, grew up, and worked among us."[18]

While Sanford may have fulfilled Zora's yearning for family ties, the community's only public school for blacks would have been a disappointment. Since the prevailing goal of black education in the Jim Crow South was to produce a compliant and well-trained workforce, the only classes offered beyond the eighth grade were vocational. So in 1912, at age twenty-one, Zora moved to the "Black Bottom" neighborhood of Nashville to live with her brother Robert and his family on his promise to send her to school if she helped his wife manage the household while he finished medical school. Two years later, in 1914, after her brother failed to keep that promise, 23-year-old Zora moved to Jacksonville to live with her brother John and his wife Blanche in Oakland (later renamed Springfield), a sprawling black middle-class neighborhood with large two-story homes and towering oak trees on the east side of Jacksonville.

Blanche's niece Mildred Murrell, who lived with John and Blanche in the early 1920s, recalls their home as a favorite place for gatherings: "The weekends were very social. John and Blanche were fond of food, music, and dancing."[19] During one of Zora's visits in 1927, she told Murrell that she was given the privacy of her own room and every consideration of the household during that short period from 1914 to 1915 when she lived with her brother. "John worked in carpentry at the time and Zora helped Blanche run a florist shop out of the front of their home," Murrell recalled.[20] Although John and his wife were good to young Zora, her irrepressible longing to pursue her education was unfulfilled. In *Dust Tracks*, she later wrote, "I had a way of life inside me and I wanted it with a want that was twisting me."[21]

What happened to cause Zora to run away from Jacksonville in 1915 to work with a traveling Gilbert and Sullivan troupe is still a mystery. Mildred Murrell remembers hearing whispers about a disappointing love affair, which may partially explain the mystery. Biographer Valerie Boyd makes a case for the same possibility, citing clues from *Dust Tracks* for support.[22] It may have been that after spending several years caring for children and working in a flower shop when what she desperately wanted was intellectual growth, Zora had decided it was time to live life on her own terms.

Regardless of what her motives were for leaving Jacksonville, it is clear that the eighteen months she spent traveling with the troupe as a maid for a performer she referred to only as "Miss M" was one of the happiest and most fulfilling periods of her life. In addition to the emotional support and friendship she received, the company provided her with the artistic, cultural, and intellectual stimulation she craved. After leaving the troupe in 1917, she moved to Baltimore to live with her sister Sarah and begin the upward climb that had so long eluded her. No longer a victim of those painful early years, at age twenty-six she enrolled in Morgan Academy to complete her high school education.

Hurston's determination to follow her mother's advice to "jump at de sun" would land her farther than she had ever imagined. After completing high school studies at Morgan, she had planned to enroll in its college program, but a happenstance meeting with Howard University student May Miller led to a loftier goal. Miller, who went on to enjoy a distinguished career as an award-winning playwright and poet, met Zora at Morgan while visiting her cousins Gwendolyn and Bernice Hughes, Hurston's classmates and friends. Miller recognized Hurston's potential and convinced her to alter her plans and shoot for Howard, the Negro Harvard.

Poised and eager to pursue her dreams, Zora moved to our nation's capital in the summer of 1918 to find work and rustle up her tuition. Before leaving Baltimore, she got word that her father had been killed when his car was hit by a train in Memphis. Having been estranged from him for many years, Zora forged ahead with her plans instead of attending his funeral and quickly found employment as a waitress at the Cosmos Club, an exclusive Washington institution that served as headquarters for the city's white male intellectual elite. Later on, she landed a job on G Street at a black-owned and -operated barbershop with a white male clientele. Strategically located near the National Press Club, the treasury department, and the Capitol, the barbershop buzzed with politicians, journalists, and businessmen whose discourse tended toward world events, national affairs, secret liaisons, and high-powered gossip.

After completing some college prep courses at Howard Academy, Hurston was finally admitted to the hallowed halls of the university she dubbed the "capstone" of African American education in 1919. On the wings of Howard University Hurston's literary star began to rise. Registering as an English major, she joined the Zeta Phi Beta sorority, participated in drama and literary activities on campus, and was awarded a coveted membership in The Stylus, Howard's prestigious literary club. Founded by professor of philosophy Alain Locke and professor of English and drama Montgomery Gregory, the club was limited to nineteen members chosen through a semiannual writing competition.

Membership in The Stylus, which published an annual journal of the same name, provided Hurston with a highly visible and respected showcase for her work. It also gained her entry into one of the greatest literary salons of the era, the home of writer Georgia Douglas Johnson. Known primarily for her poetry, Johnson hosted a weekly literary meeting at her home at 1461 S Street in Washington, D.C. Those who attended, who called themselves the "Saturday Nighters," included some of the major luminaries of what was to become the Harlem Renaissance: Alain Locke, James Weldon Johnson, Langston Hughes, Jessie Redmon Fauset, and Jean Toomer.

Hurston's first published works, a poem titled "O Night" and a short story, "John Redding Goes to Sea," appeared in The Stylus in its May 1921 issue. The short story, whose characters spoke the authentic black vernacular of Eatonville, the hallmark of her future writing, included autobiographical elements and centered on the life and death of John Redding, whose wanderlust led to his undoing. She also dabbled in poetry, writing primarily love poems, no doubt inspired in part by a handsome young Howard student named Herbert Sheen who would later become her first husband. But while *The Stylus* provided a prestigious public forum for her literary skills, it was her submissions to the Urban League's newly launched magazine *Opportunity*, based in New York, that catapulted her into a whole new realm.

While Hurston flourished at Howard, a New Negro movement was beginning to take shape in New York that was known as the Harlem Renaissance. One of its architects, *Opportunity* editor and sociologist Charles S. Johnson, used the magazine as a forum for new black literary talent. The magazine sought to lay bare the life of the Negro as it really was. At the urging of Alain Locke, Zora submitted her short story "Drenched in Light" to Johnson, who included it in the magazine's December 1924 issue. A fictionalized portrait of her early childhood in Eatonville, "Drenched in Light" marked her first nationally published short story and included ample doses of folk humor and dialect. A month after her story appeared, Johnson, profoundly impressed with her talent, persuaded Hurston to move to Harlem, which had become a mecca for black culture, drawing talented black artists from all over the world.

Hurston arrived in Harlem in January 1925, just in time to celebrate her thirty-fourth birthday. Charles S. Johnson made temporary arrangements for her to stay with his secretary, Ethel Ray, at 580 Nicolas Avenue in the affluent Sugar Hill district, where other black writers had found free food, a comfortable couch, and good company. Zora would soon be rubbing elbows with other notable black artists of the era, including singer-actress Ethel Waters and blues artist Bessie Smith.

Eventually Hurston became the most celebrated member of a cadre of bohemian black artists she famously dubbed "the Niggerati." This small, loosely knit group included writers Langston Hughes, Arna Bontemps, Countee Cullen, Wallace Thurman, Helene Johnson,

Gwendolyn Bennett, Dorothy West, and Richard Bruce Nugent. Artist Aaron Douglas, sculptor Augusta Savage, Harvard law student John P. Davis, educator Harold Jackman, and actress Dorothy Petersen were also members of the group.

Living in all-black Harlem was almost like being home in Eatonville. "At certain times I have no race, I am *me*," she observed in her self-affirming manifesto, "How It Feels to Be Colored Me," which was published in *The World Tomorrow* in May 1928. "When I set my hat at a certain angle and saunter down Seventh Ave, Harlem City, feeling as snooty as the lions in front of the Forty-Second Street Library, for instance." Obstreperously scornful of the preoccupation of her black brethren with the social burden of Negrohood, she declared: "I am not tragically colored. There is no great sorrow dammed up in my soul, nor lurking behind my eyes. . . . I do not belong to the sobbing school of Negrohood who hold that nature has somehow given them a lowdown dirty deal. . . . I am too busy sharpening my oyster knife."[23]

Hurston had plenty of reasons to feel snooty. On May 1, 1925, she was awarded two second-place prizes in *Opportunity*'s first annual literary contest: one for her short story "Spunk" and another for her play *Color Struck*. She also received honorable mentions for her short story "Black Death" and a play called *Spears*. Several months later, another short story, "Magnolia Flower," was published, in the July 25, 1925 issue of the *Spokesman*.

Having been recognized for her unique talents, Zora was now the master of her own destiny. In addition to the generosity and help afforded her by Charles Johnson, Hurston also benefited from the largesse of some of the judges of *Opportunity*'s literary contest, including writers Fannie Hurst, James Weldon Johnson, *Century* magazine editor Carl Van Doren, playwright Eugene O'Neill, actor Paul Robeson, wealthy black heiress A'Lelia Walker, philanthropist Annie Nathan Meyer, *New York Times* music critic and author Carl Van Vechten, and Alain Locke. Despite Zora's poor typing skills, Fannie Hurst gave her a job as her personal companion and secretary, and Annie Nathan Meyer, a trustee of Columbia University, procured a scholarship for her to attend Barnard College, an independent female college affiliated with Columbia University, where she studied under the supervision of renowned anthropologist Franz Boas. At Barnard, where she was the only black student, Zora was also influenced by such other giants in the anthropological field as Melville Herskovits and Ruth Benedict.

Hurston was remembered by her fellow Harlemites as much for her generosity as she was for her talent, wit, effervescence, and irreverence (she smoked cigarettes in public and wore pants, both of which were considered taboo for ladies). During the summer of 1926, the flat she rented at 43 West Sixty-Sixth Street quickly became a popular hangout for the Niggerati and was often the site of impromptu gatherings of a variety of other artists. Zora, with her Roaring '20s greased-curl hairstyle and harmonica, would drum up something good to eat and entertain her guests with hilarious southern folktales. "She was always prepared to feed people," Richard Bruce Nugent recalled.[24] She also extended her considerable generosity to friends who were in need of a place to stay or work. (Nugent himself lived with her for a time.)

In addition to her rigorous studies at Barnard, Hurston also found time to write fiction. In 1926, she published "Muttsy" in *Opportunity*, a humorous tale about a wide-eyed young woman named Pinky who moves from Eatonville to Harlem and meets Muttsy, a notorious womanizer and gambler who falls hard for her. She also published the folktale "Possum or Pig" in *Forum* and a series called "The Eatonville Anthology," a collection of history, folktales, and fiction, in *The Messenger*.

In the summer of that same year, Zora—along with close friends Langston Hughes, Wallace Thurman, Richard Bruce Nugent, Gwendolyn Bennett, John P. Davis, and Aaron Douglas—collaborated on a new magazine that would exemplify the ideals of the New Negro movement. These ideals, eloquently set forth by Hughes in his essay "The New Negro Artist and the Racial Mountain," called for an art that would cause "the smug Negro middle class to turn from their white, respectable, ordinary books and papers to catch a glimmer of their own beauty."[25]

Their quarterly magazine *Fire!* was to be a strictly artistic endeavor, one that would include articles that celebrated the black music and art of the era while allowing black artists to express themselves without inhibition or shame. Its founders' shared vision was to fill its pages with literary works by, for, and about blacks, works that were devoid of the racial commentary and propaganda that characterized its militant competitors. These included the *Crisis*, a publication of the National Association for the Advancement of Colored People (NAACP) that was edited by W. E. B. Dubois (whom Hurston later referred to as "Dr. Dubious"), and *The Messenger*, founded and edited by A. Philip Randolph and Chandler Owen.

Unfortunately, their efforts were cut short when the first issue, which included Hurston's play *Color Struck* and her short story "Sweat," failed to launch as expected. The unsold copies of *Fire!* were stored in the basement of a warehouse but were destroyed in an all-too-ironic fire.

After the first publication of *Fire!* Hurston did not publish any more fiction (other than *The First One: A Play* for Charles S. Johnson's collection *Ebony and Topaz*) until the late 1930s, taking time off to begin her formal collection of folklore, or "poking and prying with a purpose," as she phrased it. Recognizing her potential as a black southern folklorist, Boas obtained a $1,400 research fellowship for Zora to return to Florida, where she began a six-month collecting excursion that began in Jacksonville in February 1927.

There, after spending some time with her brother John and purchasing a used Ford she named "Sassy Susie," Hurston packed a chrome-plated pistol for protection and boldly moved on to other Florida cities: St. Augustine, Palatka, Sanford, and her hometown of Eatonville. As she traversed the Florida peninsula in search of folklore, she slept in her car and bravely faced the dangers a black woman traveling alone in the racist South was likely to encounter.

During her trip, she deviated from her field work only twice. She drove to Memphis to see her brother Robert. And, after living apart from her college sweetheart Herbert Sheen for five years while he attended medical school, she broke away from her research to marry him, albeit secretly. Soon after the ceremony, Sheen returned to Rush Medical College in Chicago and Zora was joined by her friend Langston Hughes. Having just completed a speaking engagement at Fisk University, he was in need of a way back to New York. "I knew it would be fun traveling with her," he later remarked. "It was."[26]

During her folklore-collecting project, Zora forged an even deeper knowledge of the South and gathered a respectable collection of folklore, but her efforts did not meet with the kind of success Boas had expected. She later relayed her disappointment in *Dust Tracks*: "I stood before Pap Franz and cried salty tears. He gave me a good going over, but later I found that he was not as disappointed as he let me think. He knew that I was green and feeling my oats, and that only bitter disappointment was going to purge me. It did."[27]

After completing her bachelor's degree in English that same year, Hurston embarked on a second, infinitely more successful attempt to gather folklore with funding provided by the sophisticated white philanthropist Charlotte Osgood Mason. The aging widow of a prominent physician, Mason, who insisted that all of her protégés call her "Godmother," was an amateur anthropologist and patron to some of Harlem's most gifted black writers, artists, and musicians, including Alain Locke, Claude McKay, Aaron Douglas, Hall Johnson, and Langston Hughes. Zora obtained funding from Mason from 1928 to 1932.

But unlike Hughes and the others who enjoyed Mason's patronage, Zora was not funded to work on her own creative or anthropological endeavors. Instead, she was under contract to work on behalf of Mason, who was no longer physically able to participate in field work. Under the terms of their agreement, Mason's funding was to remain anonymous and she was to retain exclusive rights to all of the material Hurston collected. The restriction placed on Hurston's ability to use her own material was an unfortunate circumstance, but in retrospect it is clear that Mason's patronage and genuine appreciation for the value of black culture helped Zora establish her fame as a folklorist. And though she gave a considerable amount of material to Mason,

Hurston also managed to secretly gather enough material for her own profit.

By the end of January 1928, Zora had said goodbye to Sassy Susie, purchased a more reliable Chevrolet coupe, and acquired a motion picture camera. After interviewing a former slave named Cujo Lewis in Mobile, Alabama, she headed for Florida to fulfill her contractual agreement with Mason to "collect all information possible, both written and oral, concerning the music, poetry, folk-lore, literature, hoo-doo, conjure, manifestations of art and kindred subjects relating to and existing among the north American negroes."[28] What followed was groundbreaking, adventurous, dangerous, and exciting.

For the next five years, Zora captured for future generations the very essence of black culture: its creativity, humor, and soul. She boldly traveled down the back roads of untamed Florida, living among the "Negro farthest down" in turpentine and lumber camps, citrus groves and jook joints, learning games, memorizing songs and dances, and recording folktales and ribald expressions: "Fool wid me and I'll cut all your holes into one."[29]

In hindsight, Hurston realized that her earlier attempts to collect folklore had failed primarily as a consequence of her approach: "The glamor of Barnard College was still upon me."[30] She knew where to find the material, but when she asked in her carefully accented Barnardese if anyone knew any folktales, they would simply answer negatively and direct her to the next county. Zora quickly learned to use her southern background to blend in, honing her skills so masterfully that she was able to get anyone to tell her anything even under the most stressful circumstances. But that ability only took her so far.

In a Polk County jook, where folks go "knocking the right hat off the wrong head, and backing it up with a switchblade,"[31] she was nearly stabbed by a jealous woman who had decided that Zora had gotten too friendly with her man. Hurston narrowly escaped with her life after a woman named Big Sweet, whom Zora had befriended, came to her rescue. "When the sun came up," she would remember, "I was a hundred miles up the road, headed for New Orleans."[32]

In New Orleans, a conjure stronghold, Hurston apprenticed herself to hoodoo doctors, participated in dangerous initiation ceremonies, and studied the secrets of conjure, including spells and rituals from the ceremony of death. Confident in her success, she wrote Langston Hughes, "I have landed here in the Kingdom of Marie Leveau [the city's most revered conjure queen] and expect to wear her crown someday."[33]

From New Orleans she drove south to Miami's Liberty City and discovered Bahamian dance and music that was "more original, dynamic and African" than anything she had encountered in American black culture. Intrigued with her discovery, in September she set sail for Nassau, where she was further captivated by its culture of spirit-elevating and prolific songmakers. After surviving a ferocious hurricane, she collected more than a hundred tunes and learned various kinds of "jumping dances," resolving to make them known to the world.

In the spring of 1929, armed with "more than 95,000 words of story material, a collection of children's games, conjure material, and religious material with a great number of photographs," Hurston returned to Florida and rented a small, secluded cottage near the Indian River in Eau Gallie to sort through her collection.[34] She sent some raw material to assuage an anxious Mason and, after secretly consulting with Boas, began organizing the material on lore and religion that would eventually comprise an entire issue of the *Journal of American Folklore*. Disappointed that so few people beyond the academy read it, Hurston convinced the publisher J. B. Lippincott to publish a lively revision of the material in the form of a novel, *Mules and Men*, which was published in 1935. She also wrote a skit for a play she hoped to complete in collaboration with Langston Hughes.

After embarking on a second round of folklore-collecting in the Bahamas and New Orleans, Hurston returned to New York at the end of 1929 to begin the daunting task of organizing the material she had collected for Mason into a workable manuscript. The plan was to create one comprehensive volume of conjure and folktales. Although Godmother was a strict taskmaster who adamantly insisted that Zora devote her time exclusively to her dictates, Hurston found time to begin a long-desired collaboration with Hughes on a play called *Mule Bone: A Comedy of Negro Life*. She also decided to end her marriage to Herbert Sheen, from whom she had already been separated in body as well as spirit.

Sadly, for all their good intentions, financial and authorship disputes between Hurston and Hughes turned *Mule Bone*, which was based on a humorous story Zora had heard as a child in Eatonville, into a bone of contention that eventually destroyed their deep friendship. They still continued to laugh together on occasion, but their contact remained infrequent for the rest of their lives. Ultimately, Hurston rewrote the play and retained sole authorship.

Having grown weary of trying to fashion her unwieldy folktale collection into a book, in the spring of 1931, Hurston temporarily abandoned Mason's task to write a book-length manuscript called "Barracoon," based on Cujo Lewis, the handsome, courtly former slave she had interviewed in Alabama in 1927. When Knopf editor Henry Block turned it down for publication, Hurston joined her friend Fannie Hurst on a road trip to Maine to palliate her disappointment. When the two women stopped at a whites-only Westchester County hotel for dinner, Hurst introduced her as "Princess Zora" to spare Zora the embarrassment of being turned away. Given Zora's colorful African-inspired attire, the waiter took Hurst at her word and sat them at the best table in the house. Afterward, disturbed by the need for such a shameful charade, Zora remarked to Hurst, "Who would think that a good meal could be so bitter?"[35]

By 1932, Hurston was weaning herself from Mason's financial support, but the Harlem Renaissance was winding down. The Great Depression had taken its toll across the country and the New Negro was no longer in vogue. New manuscripts went unpublished, and white patrons who had been willing and eager to invest in black artistry found other uses for their money. Charles S. Johnson had resigned as editor of *Opportunity* and, along with James Weldon Johnson, had accepted a position at Fisk University in Nashville. Countee Cullen had returned to his old high school to teach French. Langston Hughes had left Harlem for Havana, and Alain Locke had retreated to his work at Howard. Wallace Thurman died two years later in 1934 as the result of tuberculosis.

But while most of the writers in the New Negro movement had moved on, Zora still strove to showcase the "flaming glory" of authentic black art. After a collaborative effort to stage a folk revue with Hall Johnson failed to materialize, Hurston sold off her valuables, secured additional backing from Mason, and hired and trained a cast to stage her own show, *The Great Day*. The revue, which dramatized a day in the life of a Florida work camp, featured the hypnotic, rhythmic work tunes, jook songs, and games she had collected in the South. The production also included an authentic conjure ritual that had never been seen in public before. Staged at New York's John Golden Theater on January 10, 1932, it was a great success, "carried off with verve, a lack of self-consciousness, an obviously spontaneous enjoyment [that was] as eloquent as it was refreshing," one critic reported.[36] But while the show was artistically successful, it failed to render a profit, having only one run. Several months later, she assembled her cast for a second performance under a new title, *From Sun to Sun*, at The New School for Social Research.

Finding New York too expensive, Hurston moved back home to Eatonville in the summer of 1932 to find gainful employment and other possible venues for staging her production. With a cast that included some of her friends and family from Eatonville and Sanford, she staged her Florida premiere of *From Sun to Sun* at Rollins College in Winter Park on January 20, 1933. For the next few months, despite a chronic colon disorder, she presented her play in various other Florida cities to appreciative audiences, but the musical generated little, if any, profit. Godmother's last monthly check had arrived in October 1932, and Hurston was in need of income.

Mason's support and employment had been a blessing in many respects, but it was also confining. Now that her financial relationship with Mason had ended, Hurston was free to follow her own artistic compass. Hurston picked up her pen once again and completed her short story "The Gilded Six-Bits," which she sold to *Story* magazine for $20. Soon after it was featured in the magazine's August 1933 issue, Hurston received inquiries from four publishers wanting to know if she was working on any novels.

She had considered writing a novel in the past but had decided it was too risky a venture. But now, at age forty-three, she took advantage of the sudden, unexpected interest in her work. She promptly moved to Sanford and completed *Jonah's Gourd Vine*, which was quickly published by J. B. Lippincott in May 1934 as a Book-of-the-Month Club alternate selection. Largely autobiographical, set in Eatonville, and written in black southern folk dialect, her first novel was universally praised by white critics. *New York Times* critic Margaret Wallace declared: "*Jonah's Gourd Vine* can be called without fear or exaggeration the most vital and original novel about the American Negro that has yet been written by a member of the Negro race."[37] Although it was widely misread as a gross generalization of black life rather than a novel about black individuals, it was generally praised by black critics as well.[38]

Hurston was struggling to do what no other black female was attempting to do—make a living as a writer. Having to write under the constraints of white publishers was difficult for the conjure queen, who fought all of her life for the freedom to write what she wanted. Unlike her black male contemporaries W. E. B. Dubois, Richard Wright, and Sterling Brown, who were highly critical of her writing, Hurston wanted to break away from the angry black social protest literature that characterized much of their works: "I was and am thoroughly sick of the subject. My interest lies in what makes a man or a woman do such-and-so, regardless of his color."[39]

But try as she might, the small advance and meager royalties she earned were not enough to live on. (Hurston's advance on *Jonah* was a paltry $200 in comparison to Fannie Hurst's $5,000 advance for her book *Imitation of Life*.) To keep afloat, Zora had accepted an offer for a teaching position at Bethune College in January 1934 from educator and founder Mary McLeod Bethune in Daytona Beach, Florida. But that venture proved disappointing.

Hurston was expected to establish a drama department and convert an old hospital building into a workable theater. But she claimed to have difficulty even obtaining a light bulb for her office. She also found it difficult to do anything worthwhile because students were not available. She claimed that most of the 226 students enrolled in the college were already participating in established programs such as chorus, athletics, and various other dramatic groups, which left her theater program high and dry. She did manage to stage a performance of *From Sun to Sun* at the Daytona Beach Auditorium, but soon after that she abandoned the "farce" of Bethune-Cookman's drama department to pursue her own work.

In April she took a group of Bahamian dancers to St. Louis to participate in the National Folk Festival, thus securing her reputation as a respected folklorist. Her stature was also enhanced by her contributions to Nancy Cunard's anthology *Negro*, published that same spring. In her essay titled "Characteristics of Negro Expression," Hurston summarized her observations on black artistry—drama, originality, angularity, asymmetry, and a "will to adorn" (a tendency to embellish whatever they undertook). "Both prayers and sermons are tooled and polished until they are true works of art," she declared.[40] Secular language, too, was adorned with both metaphor and simile ("you sho is propaganda"), double-descriptive adjectives ("top-superior," "low-down"), and verbal nouns ("I wouldn't friend with her").[41]

Hurston continued to express her views on the intrinsic value of black folk expression in articles such as "Race Cannot Become Great Until It Recognizes Its Talents." Published in the *Washington Tribune*, a black D.C. newspaper, during the week ending December 29, 1934, it urged her black brethren to stop the "intellectual lynching" they brought upon themselves in their insistence on emulating whites. "Fawn as you will. Spend an eternity standing awe-struck," she admonished. "Roll your eyes in ecstasy and ape his every move, but until we have placed something upon his street corner that is our own, we are right back where we were when they filed our iron collars off."[42]

She went even further in an essay written the same year for the

American Mercury, a magazine edited by the journalist H. L. Mencken. In her scathing piece "You Don't Know Us Negroes," which was never published, Hurston boldly criticized the past decade of plays and novels that claimed to represent black life as "the oleomargarine era in negro writing."[43] She decried the misleading generalization and overly simplistic white view of her race, which had resulted in a decidedly warped and inaccurate portrayal of her people in literature and drama. Citing the insulting dramatic portrayal of blacks with pop-eyes as an example, she continued, "First thing on waking we laugh or skeer ourselves into another buck and wing, and so life goes."[44] Challenging both white and black artists to "treat the public to some butter," she concluded that "Negro reality is a hundred times more imaginative than anything that has ever been hatched up over a typewriter."[45]

In October 1935, Lippincott published Hurston's *Mules and Men*, a collection of folklore that included a compelling description of her hoodoo apprenticeship in New Orleans as well as Florida folktales, which she presented with their "natural juices" intact. With an introduction by Franz Boas and a dust jacket endorsement by Melville Herkovits, *Mules and Men* inspired much critical praise.

At the time of its release, Hurston was in Chicago staging a modified version of *The Great Day*. Like her previous folk revues, her revised production, *Singing Steel*, was a big success. "The vehicle, packed with folklore, drama and dancing, brings to the public not only the song and drama of a working day, but all the pathos, joy and innate feeling of freedom so characteristic of and inherent to the worker," wrote one Chicago critic.[46] The performance must have left representatives of the Julius Rosenwald Fund, who were in the audience, equally impressed; they subsequently awarded Zora a fellowship to Columbia University for a doctorate in anthropology.

But Hurston's return to Columbia did not work out exactly as planned. When the scholarship, which had originally awarded her $3,000, was reduced to $700, she stopped attending classes and concentrated on writing, taking time off for a short folklore-collecting excursion in the South with musicologist Alan Lomax and a New York University professor, Elizabeth Barnacle. And for the first time after her divorce from Herbert Sheen, Zora fell deeply in love. The object of her affection was fellow Columbia student Percival McGuire Punter, the man who was to really knock her off her feet.

Hurston had first met Punter when she cast him as a singer in her original production of *The Great Day*. Twenty-one years her junior, Punter was intelligent as well as tall, dark, and handsome. Although destined to be the "real love" of her life, Punter was unable to accept Zora's unconventional lifestyle. He refused to accompany her to literary parties and resented her going without him. He was jealous and possessive, and when he asked her to give up her career and marry him, Hurston broke it off.

When her relationship with Punter fell apart, Hurston turned her attention to making a living. The Great Depression was still gripping the nation and jobs were hard to come by. Given the dire circumstances, Hurston and many other artists of the period found employment through the Works Progress Administration (WPA), one of President Roosevelt's ambitious relief programs. After working six months with greats such as John Houseman and Orson Welles as an employee in the "Negro Unit" of the WPA's Federal Theater Project in New York, Hurston set out to study voodoo in Jamaica and Haiti in the spring of 1936 with a grant she had received from the Guggenheim Foundation.

At this juncture in her life, the purpose behind her folklore-collecting moved away from the scientific spyglass of anthropological research to scientific observations for the purposes of creating fiction that "shall give a true picture of Negro Life," as stated on her Guggenheim Foundation application.[47] The acclaim she had received for *Mules and Men* and her folk revues had cemented her reputation as a folklorist and anthropologist. But writing was her first love, and she had decided to pursue it with all deliberate speed.

Hurston spent six months in Jamaica learning about the poisons used by the voodoo and bush doctors and living among the Maroons in Accompong, where she studied with their chief conjure doctor. In September 1936, she moved on to Port-au-Prince, Haiti, and rented a small house in the suburbs. Within a few months she had earned the trust of the secretive voodoo priests, also known as two-headed doctors, who provided her with a working knowledge of the major voodoo gods. She gathered reams of glorious folklore and established eight authentic cases of zombies. As a result of her research, she was the first anthropologist to identify voodoo as a bona fide religion. After spending a brief time in New York in March, Hurston returned to Haiti to delve further into its voodoo rituals (particularly the secret behind the making of zombies), eventually becoming an initiate.

In addition to her research, Zora took seven weeks while in Haiti to pen her second and most celebrated novel, *Their Eyes Were Watching God*. Drawing inspiration from the deep love and passion she had known with Punter, the story, set in Florida, follows the life of Janie Crawford, a beautiful mulatto, as she wrestles against the restraints of class, womanhood, marriage, and race to find her own identity and the love of her life, nicknamed Tea Cake.

Almost succumbing to a violent gastric disturbance from drinking contaminated water, Hurston abandoned her research and returned to the states just as Lippincott's release of *Their Eyes* was receiving rave reviews. On September 26, 1937, in a review titled "Vibrant Book Full of Nature and Salt," Sheila Hibben, a *New York Herald Tribune* critic, called it a "lovely book" by "an author that writes with her head as well as with her heart."[48]

But while her white audience, black women, and critics lauded the book, which is now considered a masterpiece in the canons of American and African American literature, most of her black male contemporaries were not so impressed. While black writers such as George Schuyler responded positively to the novel, Richard Wright, future author of the 1940 social protest novel *Native Son*, acknowledged Zora's literary gift but accused her of exploiting and "perpetuating the minstrel image" for her white readership.[49] Writing for the January 1938 issue of *Opportunity*, Alain Locke praised *Their Eyes* for its poetry, dialect, and humor but complained that it lacked a deep "inner psychology" and "analysis of the social background."[50]

Undaunted by their lack of appreciation for her folk-inspired fiction, Hurston was stalwart in her resistance to the pressures from her black male contemporaries to rehash the race issue. She believed that black writers who followed the path of the "Race Champions" did so to the detriment of art.

After taking some time to organize her material from Jamaica and Haiti into what would become her fourth published book and second folklore collection, *Tell My Horse* (1938), Zora worked briefly for another WPA program, the Florida Writers' Project (FWP). The aim of the FWP, which functioned under the auspices of the Federal Writers' Project, was to employ writers, editors, and field workers to produce a state tourism guide. Although infinitely more qualified than any of the state's supervisory and editorial staff, Hurston was first hired as a fieldworker in the "Negro Unit" to collect information for the African American histories component at a meager monthly salary of $75. She was ultimately reassigned to an informal position as editor of *The Florida Negro* section and given a raise to $142 per month, but only after Henry Alsberg, the national project director, intervened.[51]

In addition to her editing duties, Hurston, working primarily from a cabin in Eatonville, undertook brief folklore recording expeditions in the far-flung turpentine camps of Florida. One of the camps, located in White Springs, was owned and operated by the Bullard family. It was one of the largest camps in Florida, housing approximately 75 to 100 black families. Like most turpentine camps, the workers lived in clapboard cottages with small front porches. There were no windows or electricity, only shutters and kerosene lamps. During Hurston's visit, Mary Bullard, the family matriarch, gave her lodging in a large two-story wooden farmhouse located near the camp. The late-nineteenth-century home, which also served as the residence of the family's black cook, had eight working fireplaces and a wraparound porch.[52]

According to her grandson Johnnie, Mary Bullard was quite taken with Zora, describing her as an "intelligent, effervescent person who loved to laugh."[53] Upon Hurston's departure, noting Zora's affinity for stylish hats, Mary gave her a cranberry-colored velvet toque that was gathered on one side with an ostrich plume and pin.[54]

Zora also undertook a brief folklore recording expedition in the turpentine camps of Cross City, Florida, with photographer Bob Cook, state editor William Duncan, and musicologist Alan Lomax. She contributed copious amounts of her own writings to *The Florida Negro*, including "The Sanctified Church," "Turpentine," "Art and Such," "Go Gator and Muddy the Water," and "New Children's Games." Incredibly, when the final manuscript was published in 1993 as *The Florida Negro: A Federal Writers' Project Legacy*, all of Hurston's writings were omitted.

Before leaving her job with the Florida Writers' Project, Hurston married her second husband, 23-year-old Albert Price, III, on June 27, 1939, in Fernandina Beach, Florida. Price, the son of a prominent Jacksonville family, was an employee of the WPA education department. Hurston, then forty-eight, shaved nineteen years off her actual birth date, listing it on her marriage license as 1910. But her new union lasted only six weeks.

Realizing her mistake, Hurston left Price and accepted a teaching position in Durham at the North Carolina College for Negroes, where she hoped to create a production company dedicated to the presentation of folk life. Shortly after she arrived, she was invited to be the only black member of a dramatic writing seminar taught by Chapel Hill professor and Pulitzer Prize–winning playwright Paul Green. During these sessions, Hurston and Green discussed a collaborative effort, a play she had been working on titled *High John De Conquer*.

She also took the time to promote her new novel, *Moses, Man of the Mountain*, her fifth book and third novel, which she had completed while working for the Florida Writers' Project. It was released on November 2. *Moses* was a brilliant retelling of the story of Moses and his people in the Negro idiom as an allegorical representation of black America's struggle for freedom.

Hurston was thrilled when *Moses* generated mostly positive reviews, but she was not so content with her formal teaching position. Finding herself at odds with the institution's code of behavior, on March 1, 1940, Zora left her teaching position mid-semester to assist anthropologists Margaret Mead and Jane Belo in a study of religious trances in various cultures, including Bali and Haiti. For purposes of comparison, they wanted to study religious behavior in a sanctified church. To that end, Belo hired Hurston, at a salary of $150 a month, to conduct a two-month study of ecstatic religious behavior in the West African Gullah culture in Beaufort, South Carolina. Gullah's rich black cultural heritage includes a long history of slavery that began hundreds of years ago when the first captive West Africans were transported in chains across the Atlantic Ocean and forced to work on Beaufort's prosperous indigo and rice plantations.

When Belo briefly joined Hurston in April, Zora took her to Rev. George Washington's Commandment Keeper Seventh Day Church, where the keynote was rhythm; the church had rattle gourds, guitars, washboards, cymbals, and tambourines. Zora recorded interviews with the communicants, who provided stories and vivid descriptions of their visions and conversion experiences, which were later recorded in Hurston's scholarly unpublished essay, "Ritualistic Expression from the Lips of the Communicants of the Seventh Day Church of God." After visiting several other churches in the area, Belo returned to New York, leaving Zora to continue the study.

At Zora's request, Belo sent two filmmakers and the necessary equipment to film numerous church services, a baptism, and other ceremonies. In one of the scenes from the footage, which begins with an animated sermon followed by the prophesying of a woman in a trance, Zora can be seen playing the maracas in accompaniment with others who are playing cymbals, guitars, and tambourines. Hurston also made her own recording, which she hoped to use in her collaboration with Paul Green on *High John De Conquer*, but Green bowed out of the deal, opting instead to work with Richard Wright on a stage adaptation of his bombshell novel *Native Son*.

After completing her work in Beaufort, Hurston briefly returned to New York. Then, in the spring of 1941 she moved to California to work as a writer and technical advisor for Paramount Studios and to begin working on her autobiography. During her stay, she was the houseguest of her wealthy white friend and anthropologist Katherine Edson Mershon, who took her on a sightseeing tour of the state. By the end of July, at the urging of her publisher, Zora had finished the first draft of her autobiography *Dust Tracks on a Road* and published a short story that mocked the idea of racial purity, "Cock Robin Beale Street," in the *Southern Literary Messenger*.

When the Japanese bombed Pearl Harbor, Zora decided it was prudent to leave the West Coast and return to Florida. After resigning her position at Paramount, she moved to St. Augustine in January 1942, where she met and befriended writer Marjorie Kinnan Rawlings and secured a teaching position at Florida Normal and Industrial College. In addition to her teaching responsibilities, she managed not only to revise and submit to Lippincott *Dust Tracks* (which garnered harsh criticism but also won her kudos and celebrity status when it was released that same year) but also to publish her coded, sexually charged story about two Harlem pimps, "Story in Harlem Slang," in the July 1942 issue of *American Mercury*.

A brief reconciliation with her husband Albert Price revealed him to be, in Zora's eyes, a man of dubious character. So on October 2, 1942, she informed him of her intentions to obtain a divorce in a caustic and biting (and until now unpublished) letter, which she began with "Dear Albert":

Here is my ring. By putting it into your hands, I hope this makes it unnecessary for you to come to see me for any reason what so ever. In fact, it is my earnest prayer that I never see you again, unless you are dead. If you will only be decent enough to die, I will buy me a red dress, send myself some flowers of congratulations, and come to your funeral. So, I do not expect you to come near me, to write me, nor to phone me, nor to send me messages by word of mouth. I shall take the police to see to it, that I am not annoyed. I have no business to even know anybody like you, and I never would have, either, if you had not lied your way into my life. You knew that I would not have any inmate of a sporting house (you have admitted as much to me) and that is why you lied both by words and by hiding the truth from me to get me to marry you. That is why your stupid mind told you to try to get me to take you away from Jacksonville immediately after the marriage so I would not find out. If I had known as much about you then as I know now, I never would have wasted my time and nerve doing it then. But I thought you had some decency, which I know now that you have not.[55]

The marriage between Price and Hurston, which they largely spent apart from one another, was formally ended by a divorce granted on November 9, 1943.

Now the most published black woman in America, Hurston was at the top of her game. After the success of *Dust Tracks*, she was profiled in *Current Biography* and *Who's Who*. She was also commissioned to write two more articles for the lily-white, middle-class *Saturday Evening Post* and to contribute additional pieces to *American Mercury* and *Reader's Digest*.

When she won the prestigious Anisfield-Wolf Book Award in 1943 for *Dust Tracks*, Hurston used the $1,000 prize money to buy a 32-foot houseboat she named *Wanago*. Having left St. Augustine and moved to Daytona Beach earlier in the year, she berthed her boat at Howard's Boat Works, located on the Halifax River, and remained happily planted in Daytona until the end of 1943. The white owner's daughter, Elizabeth Howard, who was then a young child, remembered visiting Zora from time to time and being captivated by her folktales. "Zora's houseboat was made of wood, and it floated gently on the water like the little ark pictured in my Bible stories," she recalled.[56] "Inside the cabin were windows all around. I would sit at a little table and Zora would be sitting across from me."[57] Howard doesn't recall how many times she visited Zora, but her persona left a lasting impression. "I only remember one of her stories, a folktale about how black people got black. The day Zora told me that story she was wearing a brown turban. I loved Zora's stories, and I loved Zora."[58]

Hurston loved the solitude of life on the water. Taking advantage of the quietude, she devoted most of her time to writing essays and articles for *American Mercury*. Her essay on the complicated relationship between whites and blacks in the South, "The Pet Negro System," was published in May 1943. Another essay, "High John de Conquer," which was based on a folktale and praised the redeeming powers of love and laughter to overcome oppression, was published in October, while her article "Negroes without Self-Pity" was featured in the November issue.

When she wasn't writing or doing periodic speaking engagements, Hurston indulged her love of reading and of boating. Some of her favorite authors included Mark Twain, Charles Dickens, Robert Nathan, Anatole France, Anne Morrow Lindbergh, Sinclair Lewis, and Willa Cather. She was also interested in the Chinese philosophy of Taoism and the teachings of Dutch philosopher Benedict de Spinoza. More at home in the water than on land, Zora made time for leisurely trips up and down the St. John's and Halifax rivers, visiting family and friends along the way. She also became a member of the Florida Negro Defense Committee, a local civil rights group that did not see blacks as victims and gave talks to segregated audiences of GIs as part of the Recreation in War program sponsored by Mary Holland, Florida governor Spessard Holland's wife.

On January 18, 1944, at age fifty-three, Hurston, married for the third and final time (though she claimed to be forty on her marriage license). Her new husband, 45-year-old James Howell Pitts, a resident of Brunswick, Georgia. Soon after the wedding in Volusia County, Florida, Zora left her new husband to travel to New York to work with Dorothy Waring, the wife of a theatrical producer, on a new musical called *Polk County*. Inspired by the characters she had met there, the play's main character was to be Hurston's old jook pal, Big Sweet. Since the material was ostensibly Zora's, it seems likely that the primary reason she would have agreed to collaborate with Waring was to appease Waring's theatrical producer husband, who was more likely to produce the play if his wife had a hand in it. After a brief collaboration that was plagued with artistic differences, Hurston returned to her houseboat for the rest of the summer. But like her previous unions, her marriage to Pitts was short lived, ending in divorce on October 31, 1944.

In the year that followed, Hurston survived a tonsillectomy and a hurricane; replaced the weathered *Wanago* with a new boat, the *Sun*

Tan; and began working on several manuscripts and a novel, all of which were ultimately rejected. To generate income, she also continued her journalistic writing, publishing several essays. One of these essays, "Crazy for This Democracy," published in the December 1945 issue of *Negro Digest*, is considered the most politically honest piece of journalism Hurston wrote in the 1940s. It was written at the close of World War II and refers to the inherent hypocrisy in the late President Roosevelt's boast that America was "the arsenal of democracy." Hurston pondered whether the president meant to say America's "Ass-and-All" democracy. If so, she argued, it would have certainly been a more honest appraisal of a country whose foreign policy supports democracy abroad while "subjugating the dark world completely" through its sanctioning of Jim Crow laws at home.

Over the next few years, Hurston sold her houseboat, lived briefly in Harlem, traveled to Honduras, and completed her last novel, *Seraph on the Suwannee*. By 1948, at age fifty-seven, she had survived the tragedies and losses of her early years and triumphed over the barriers of race, class, and gender to excel beyond even her wildest dreams as a writer, anthropologist, and folklorist. She held degrees from prestigious Howard University and Barnard College, where she had studied under the direction of renowned anthropologist Franz Boas. She had been the recipient of a Guggenheim research grant, a Rosenwald Fellowship, and an Anisfield-Wolf Book Award. Her groundbreaking anthropological research and folklore-collecting had taken her to the far (and often perilous) reaches of the American Deep South, Jamaica, Honduras, the Bahamas, and Haiti, and she had become an initiate of the voodoo religion. During the 1920s, as a central figure in the Harlem Renaissance, she wrote award-winning plays and short stories and helped shape the aesthetic paradigm of the New Negro movement. She had staged the nation's first authentic black folk performances, worked as a script consultant for Paramount Studios, and garnered the admiration and friendship of some of the nation's most respected wordsmiths: Langston Hughes, Countee Cullen, James Weldon Johnson, Carl Sandburg, Marjorie Kinnan Rawlings, Fannie Hurst, and the white impresario of black culture, Carl Van Vechten. In addition to her short stories and plays, her published works included numerous articles, an autobiography, two books on folklore, and three novels; she was awaiting the publication of her fourth.

Hurston's ups and downs, gains and losses, successes and failures had woven a yarn as colorful as any of the tales she had penned. Yet, as remarkable as her life had been (and would continue to be), nothing could have prepared her for the horror she would face in the fall of 1948, an event so devastating that it almost destroyed her.

1

IN HELL'S BASEMENT

Harlem, 1948–1949

*My Country has failed me utterly. My race has seen fit to
destroy me without reason, and with the vilest tools conceived
of by man so far . . . I feel hurled down a filthy privy hole.*

Hurston's nightmare began Monday, September 13, 1948 with an unexpected knock on the door of her rented room at West 112th Street in Harlem. Charles Scribner's Sons' publication of her fourth and latest novel, *Seraph on the Suwanee*, was only a month away, and her immediate concern was its success. But that concern vanished when she opened the door to a New York City police detective who had come to arrest her on one of the vilest charges imaginable—child molestation. The charges, which were unequivocally false, had been filed by the Children's Society on behalf of Mayme Allen, Hurston's former landlady, after her ten-year-old son Billy claimed that Zora and two other adults had sexually abused him and two of his friends. Zora had rented a room in Allen's Harlem residence at 425 West 124th Street from October 1946 to May 1947. Billy alleged that the abuse had occurred the following year, which would have been impossible as Hurston was in Honduras and upstate New York at that time. Zora categorically denied the charges and offered to take a lie detector test, but to no avail. Despite her protests, she was arrested, interrogated, and booked into jail during what must have been a horrific few hours.

Within hours of her arrest, Scribner's sent Zora's editor and friend Burroughs Mitchell and attorney Louis Waldman to make arrangements for her release. After spending the better part of the day in a jail cell, she spent the night at the home of Mitchell and his wife, who did all they could to reassure and comfort her. The following morning, at her arraignment, a brief hearing before a magistrate and her accusers to hear and answer to the charges, Hurston maintained her innocence and requested a preliminary hearing, a legal proceeding in which a judge decides whether enough credible evidence exists to support the charges.

Louis Waldman, whose $1,000 attorney's fee was paid by Scribner's and charged against Zora's future royalties from *Seraph*, represented her at the preliminary hearing on September 21, 1948. Determined to prove her innocence beyond a shadow of a doubt, Zora appeared in court with confidence and dignity wearing a scarf of bright red, her signature color. Waldman, who was convinced of her innocence, was incredulous that the Children's Society had failed to investigate the accusations before initiating legal action. Had the society bothered to conduct an investigation, Hurston's passport and other evidence would have exonerated her. More disturbing yet was the fact that the society had set August 15th as the one definitive date when the molestation was supposed to have occurred and set it after Zora had given the dates and times she was out of the country to society official Alexander Miller. "Then the horror took me," she told a friend, "for I saw that he [Miller] was not seeking the truth, but to make his charges stick. . . . I could not believe that this was happening in the United States and least of all to me."[1]

During the hearing, District Attorney Frank Hogan presented no evidence other than the lurid testimony of the three boys. Billy claimed that he and his friends had met Hurston and the other adults (whom she had never met) every Saturday afternoon at 4:30 for almost two years in the basement of a West 124th Street building and were paid 50 cents to allow one of the adults to have oral sex with them while the others watched. Only one of the other adults, a black male janitor, was formally charged. The third defendant, a Hispanic mother of four who owned a nearby candy store, was not arrested.

To Hurston's growing astonishment, this travesty of justice was not only playing out on American soil to an innocent, law-abiding citizen but in Harlem City, among her own people: "Please do not forget that this thing was not done in the South, but in the so-called liberal North. Where shall I look for justice?"[2] After selling her house boat, the *Sun-tan*, in the fall of 1946, Hurston had left Florida and headed north in hope of drumming up some freelance work in New York City. Soon after, she was drawn into Harlem's political arena and began working for the congressional campaign of Republican candidate Grant Reynolds, who was ultimately defeated by incumbent Adam Clayton Powell. Ironically, Zora told friend Carl Van Vechten that she had remained in Harlem after the election because New York City had become "too much of a basement to hell" where people had become "busy hating and speaking in either brazen lies or using just enough truth to season a lie up to make their viewpoint sound valid."[3] But she escaped one hell only to be entrapped by another.

Looking back, Hurston could find little to explain why the boys would concoct such a sordid tale. During the few months she had lived in Allen's building, she wrote several articles for various newspapers and became actively engaged in her community. In an effort to improve the lives of the families in her neighborhood, she organized a "Black Mothers" initiative, a popular arrangement whereby nonworking women took turns caring for the children of the working mothers on their block free of charge. She wrote book reviews for the *New York Herald Tribune*, including ones written by her anthropological colleagues: *Journey to Accompong* by Katherine Dunham and *Trinidad Village* by Melville and Frances Herkovits. She also wrote two satirical essays that were never published: "The Lost Keys of Glory," on the role of women, and "Back to the Middle Ages," on the evils of communism.

Billy Allen was widely known as a troubled youth, and Hurston had advised his mother to take him to Bellevue Hospital for psychological evaluation and treatment, which she did for a time. But this vile hoax went far beyond what Zora thought him capable of: "The thing is too fantastic, too evil, too far from reality for me to conceive of it."[4]

Two women who lived in Hurston's former neighborhood, Mrs. Ryan and Mrs. Davis, believed that Billy's mother might have been involved in the ruse. In a conversation with Zora, the women revealed that shortly before the allegations against her were made, Mayme Allen confessed to them that she had caught Billy engaging in homosexual acts with Jerry, one of Hurston's accusers, and was desperate to get rid of her son.[5] Additionally, Billy's aberrant behavior was a constant source of trouble, and the (married) man with whom Allen was living deeply disliked him. When her efforts to enroll Billy in boarding school failed, she resolved to try to have him committed. Ryan and Davis suspected that Allen may have concocted the molestation claims to strengthen her case for her son's commitment while placing the blame for his corruption on Hurston and the others.[6] Mayme Allen later admitted to the district attorney that she disliked and resented Zora, which no doubt made her a convenient target.

Whether or not Allen was behind the scam is unknown, but the truth surrounding Billy's homosexual encounters was revealed during the preliminary hearing, when he admitted to Louis Waldman on cross-examination that he and the other two plaintiffs frequently met in the basement on Saturdays to have intercourse. But rather than explore the implications of these facts, Francis X. Giaccone, the presiding magistrate, ruled that a criminal trial would go forward. Hurston was arraigned on October 11 and charged with one count of assault in the second degree, three counts of sodomy, and one count of "placing a child in such a situation as likely to impair morals."[7]

Bolstered by the successful launch of her new novel and her attorney's assurances of a swift acquittal, Hurston remained cautiously optimistic. Because the case involved minors, the proceedings had been confidential, and the release of *Seraph* (on the same day she was indicted) was met by brisk sales and good reviews. After selling the initial 3,000 copies during the first few days of publication, Scribner's had to print 2,000 additional copies to keep up with demand. One reviewer, a critic for the *New York Herald Tribune*, praised Hurston for her "astonishing, bewildering talent" and described *Seraph* as "emotional, expository; meandering, unified, naive, sophisticated; sympathetic, caustic; comic, tragic, lewd, chaste—one could go on indefinitely reiterating this novel's contradictions and still end helplessly with the adjective unique."[8] In light of its success, Scribner's offered Zora a $500 advance on an option to publish her next novel.

Seraph on the Suwanee was Hurston's first attempt to write about poor whites in defiance of what she referred to as "that old silly rule about Negroes not writing about white people."[9] Scholars have suggested various reasons for this bold move, but one of the most obvious seems to have been her strong desire for commercial success.[10] J. B. Lippincott, her previous publisher, had turned down her last two manuscripts about black life, and she was weary of investing her time and resources on manuscripts that were ultimately rejected. Moreover, African American writers such as Ann Petry and Chester Himes had achieved moderate success depicting white characters. Her decision was also influenced by her friend, Florida writer Marjorie Kinnan Rawlings, who had successfully written about poor southern whites. Her classic novel *The Yearling* (1938) earned Rawlings a Pulitzer Prize, and in 1941 MGM Studios made a film version of the story starring Gregory Peck and Jane Wyman.

Set in rural Florida and dedicated to her friends Rawlings and Mary Holland, *Seraph* chronicles the life of "cracker born and bred" Arvay Henson and her marriage to an attractive, enterprising, albeit deeply chauvinistic husband, Jim Meserve (Hurston calls him Me Serve). Much like Janie Crawford, the black protagonist in *Their Eyes Were Watching God*, Arvay, a victim of her gender and of the mores and values of her poor white social class, embarks on a quest for self-fulfillment and love despite these obstacles and her own troubled misconceptions and insecurities. But unlike Janie, who discovers her own unique voice, Arvay ultimately realizes her self-worth only in relation to her husband's love of and need for her.

The dialogue, written in the idiom of the backwoods white southerner, echoed a similar cadence and musicality to that inherent in the language of rural black folk, but it lacked the more elaborate metaphors spoken by the black characters in her previous novels. In reference to the origin of the Meserves' language, Hurston told Rawlings: "About the idiom of the book, I too thought that when I went out to dwell among the poor white in Dixie County that they were copying us. But I found their colorful speech so general that I began to see that Negroes introduced into N. America spoke *no* English at all, and learned from whites. Our sense of rhythm points it up a bit, but the expressions for the most part are English held over from the Colonial period."[11]

Although none of Hurston's novels were made into films during her lifetime, they were seriously considered by several major studios. *Seraph* was reviewed in galleys by MGM and Warner Brothers and won favorable reactions from both. Warner Brothers considered it a story with "tried and true" elements that would be relatively inexpensive to film and thought it might be a possible vehicle for actress Jane Wyman. Kenneth Mackenna of MGM was equally impressed with the book's potential for film adaptation, describing the story as refreshing and "delightful."[12] Warner Brothers also reviewed *Their Eyes Were Watching God*, and several studios reviewed her autobiography, *Dust Tracks on a Road*, as soon as it was published.[13] To date, only one of Hurston's novels has been adapted into film. *Their Eyes* was produced by Oprah Winfrey in 2004 as a made-for-television-movie starring Halle Berry.

Given *Seraph*'s success, her publisher's advance, and her attorney's assurances, Hurston had plenty of reasons to celebrate, but her well-placed optimism was short lived. Because juvenile case records were kept sealed, Hurston believed that she would at least be spared any bad publicity, but she was dead wrong. In October, a meddling black court employee leaked Billy's story to two black newspapers, which both ran stories: the *New York Age* and the Baltimore-based *Afro-American*. When Bill Chase, a reporter for the *New York Age*, caught up to a "hysterical" Zora, she adamantly denied the "impossible accusation" and assured the reporter that her passport would prove her innocence.[14] His story, "Noted Novelist Denies She 'Abused' 10-Year-Old-Boy," appeared in *Age* on October 23, 1948.

Chase's story, however balanced, was humiliating enough, but the crowning blow was delivered by the *Afro-American*, which never interviewed her or investigated the facts. Instead, on the same day Chase's story saw print, the *Afro-American* ran a salacious account of the charges in its national edition under one gigantic headline, "Boys 10, Accuse Zora," and three smaller ones, including: "Novelist Arrested in Morals Charge." To capitalize on the story, the article quoted dialogue from *Seraph* out of context, combining it with a reviewer's statement to make their reporting all the more lurid: "Reviewer of Author's Latest Book Notes Character Is 'Hungry for Love,'" and "Did She Want 'Knowing and Doing' Kind of Love?"[15] To further titillate, the articles were accompanied by an old photo of Zora wearing a low-cut dress and smiling mischievously.

The public lynching by the *Afro-American* devastated Hurston almost to the point of suicide. In a letter written in the throes of despair, she told Van Vechten: "No acquittal will persuade some people that I am innocent. . . . All that I have believed in has failed me. I have resolved to die."[16] Fortunately, given life-sustaining moral and financial support from Burroughs Mitchell, Fannie Hurst, Marjorie Kinnan Rawlings, and Carl Van Vechten and her own unrelenting determination to survive, Hurston did not succumb to her temporary state of despondency. Upon receiving a letter from Fannie Hurst during her darkest hours, Hurston replied: "Thanks for your magnificence of spirit. Your thrust of light reached me in my cave so dark and deep that it seems that all the suns of the universe cannot light it up."[17]

But just as she regained her balance, she was hit by another blow. In January 1949, Richard Rochester, a white Harlem GOP leader whom Zora had met while working on the Reynolds congressional campaign, launched a personal vendetta against her after she refused to become involved in a small claims suit he had brought against one of her male acquaintances. The suit alleged that the man owed Rochester $270.15 for a car he had sold him. When the man refused to pay it, Rochester filed a claim against him and asked Hurston to testify on his behalf even though she knew nothing of the transaction. Hurston told her attorney, Louis Waldman, that when she refused to perjure herself, Rochester "threatened me with a nation-wide bath of filthy publicity."[18] (Rochester lost the case.)

Intent on revenge, Rochester, who was white, followed through on his threat by contacting several black newspapers, including the *Afro-American*, as well as Scribner's and *New York World-Telegram* columnist Helen Worden Erskine to claim that Zora owed him $20 from a loan and $275 for damages sustained to his car after he had lent it to her. He also accused her of indecent exposure and illegal marijuana use, which was reported in the *Afro-American*.[19] He even went so far as to peddle his lies in small claims court, filing suit against her for the $270, and he later told the *Afro-American* that she had illegally registered to vote in both New York and Florida.[20] Hurston and her attorney saw through his ploy, which was clearly staged to generate damaging publicity before the sodomy trial, and easily defeated him in his small claims suit on February 9, 1949.

Hurston was undoubtedly relieved to be rid of Rochester's spurious suit, but the satisfaction of defeating him likely paled in comparison to the larger victory she anticipated. Around the middle of March, the New York City district attorney announced that after further investigation and a review of Hurston's passport, his office had concluded that she was innocent. Unbeknown to Zora, during the investigation in November, Billy Allen had already admitted that he had invented the story to shield himself from punishment after his mother discovered his homosexual activity and that the other boys had backed him up. After reading the district attorney's seven-page report and recommendation, the judge officially dismissed the charges against Zora and the other defendants on March 14, 1949.

The dismissal of the case spared Zora from the humiliation of a trial, but the damage to her reputation and career was already done. Even her innocence had been powerless against the sordid news accounts of a black press more concerned with profit than with fact. During the months that followed, she lived in a kind of hellish limbo, avoiding the press and battling depression. She kept to herself but continued to correspond with the friends and family members whose love and support had sustained her throughout her ordeal. She managed to complete her short story "Conscience of the Court" and a book review for the *New York Herald Tribune*, but her subsequent efforts to begin her new novel "The Lives of Barney Turk" were thwarted by too many distractions or, as she put it, "a severe case of paper poisoning."[21]

To add to her woes, the room she had rented in the Bronx was noisy and cramped and lacked a telephone. Left only with the hope that her short story would sell, she accepted her plight with reluctant resignation: "I am terribly unhappy where I am situated, but until I hear from my agent, here I am, and no help for it."[22] But help did come toward the end of May when the *Saturday Evening Post* purchased "Conscience of the Court" for $900.

After suffering through one of the most difficult times of her life, Hurston wanted nothing more than to put New York and the horrors she had faced behind her and resume the anthropological research she had begun in Honduras in the late 1940s. Now, with the means at hand, she could begin making plans. Her fascination with the Central American country had been inspired in September 1944 by a mining engineer named Reginald Brett, who had spent several years mining in the region. When Brett returned to the states and read Hurston's *Tell My Horse* (1938), he had sought her out to tell her that he had seen an ancient Mayan ruin in the Honduran jungle that no other white person had set eyes upon. Impressed with Hurston's research, Brett had urged her to find this hidden archeological treasure and explore the country's plentiful, virgin folklore.

Brett's challenge had set Hurston's imagination on fire. Eager to get the ball rolling, she had called Henry Allen Moe of the Guggenheim Foundation to seek funds for the trip, asked friend and adventurer Fred Irvine to provide transportation on his schooner, and invited Jane Belo, a friend and fellow anthropologist, to accompany her. Her plans had been to locate and study the lost Mayan ruins and to live among and collect folklore from the Paya, Zambu, Mayan, and Carib Indians. When the Guggenheim Foundation had refused her request, she had spent the next two years raising the money herself and had finally sailed to Honduras alone on a commercial liner on May 14, 1947. She remained in Honduras for eight months, but her research had been cut short by the onslaught of the Honduran rainy season and the need to complete *Seraph*.

Feeling betrayed by both her race and her country, it is no wonder that Hurston was anxious to return to Central America. To arrange transportation, she contacted her friend Fred Irvine, who now owned a cargo ship, *The Challenger*. The Englishman and adventurer agreed to make the voyage if he could procure enough cargo to finance the trip. In the meantime, he offered Hurston a peaceful refuge on his vessel, which was anchored in the aquamarine waters of Miami's Biscayne Bay. In September, Zora enthusiastically accepted his offer and headed south toward the healing rays of the Florida sun.

2

SUNSHINE AND
SOUTHERN POLITICS

Miami, 1950

Way over there, where the sun rises a day ahead of time,
they say that heaven arms with love and laughter
those it does not wish to see destroyed.

Hurston returned to her home state at a pivotal time in the history of the South and the nation. The decade of the '50s ushered in the beginning of the Cold War with Russia and signaled a challenge to the nation to extend to all its citizens the social, economic, and political freedoms guaranteed under the U.S. Constitution and fought for in World War II. President Harry S. Truman responded to the challenge with proposals for civil rights legislation, which the South bitterly opposed. By June 1950, NAACP attorney Thurgood Marshall had won three cases before the Supreme Court, including one that struck down segregation in higher education and was planning an all-out legal attack on public school segregation.

These victories came on the heels of the 1944 Supreme Court ruling in *Smith v. Albright*, which declared the South's practice of excluding blacks from voting in "whites only" primaries unconstitutional. In the wake of this decision, the Ku Klux Klan went on a rampage of cross-burning terrorism to keep blacks away from the polls, while southern state legislatures concocted new ways to circumvent the Court's ruling. Black citizens who tried to vote in the South risked loss of employment, retaliatory violence, or even death.

This highly charged political and social atmosphere would eventually draw Zora into one of the most notorious Senate campaigns in U.S. history and inspire some of her most spirited and controversial political and social commentary. But for the time being she was anxious to begin work on her new novel and enjoy some much-needed rest and recuperation on Irvine's boat before setting out for Honduras.

Hurston described 31-year-old Fred Irvine as a "faithful friend." Born in England and raised in New York, the ruggedly good-looking and artistic Irvine had become a bohemian adventurer after his father died and left him an inheritance. Zora was grateful for his accommodations and elated to be home again, but she was deeply disappointed to find *The Challenger* in great disorder from bow to stern, a condition that was reflected in its captain's turbulent emotional state. In a letter to her editor at Scribner's, Burroughs Mitchell, she confided that Irvine, the quintessential ladies' man, was suffering from a string of love affairs that had soured his soul and was counting on her wit and wisdom to buoy him up: "Maybe because he is a small guy and unsure of himself in other ways that he feels that he must promote all those meaningless 'love' affairs to make him feel assured."[1] In a grand gesture of friendship, a weary Hurston put aside her own emotional needs and lent Irvine a sympathetic ear and an experienced pair of deck hands. When *The Challenger* was again shipshape, he repaid her with a soul-soothing cruise to the Bahamas. Upon their return, Zora settled in as the ship's "supercargo" and resumed work on her new novel while Irvine scouted for business and gambled, often with money he had borrowed from her.

For Hurston, life on the water, flanked by the sun-drenched tropical landscape, proved a potent elixir. The location of *The Challenger*, which was anchored along the MacArthur Causeway (which connects the Florida mainland to Miami's South Beach), offered some of the city's most spectacular views. Zora, child of the sun, was in her element. In the pink hours of the early morning, she walked to a nearby park to gather sun-ripened coconuts and star fruit. And she never missed the opportunity to be topside at sunset, marveling at the spectacular stroke of nature's paintbrush emblazoned across the sky: "And God keeps His appointment with Miami every sundown."[2] Having recovered life's cadence once again, she told Mitchell, "I feel that I have come to myself at last."[3] Even her bitterness toward her race over the scandal had begun to soften: "I can even endure the sight of a Negro, which I thought once I could never do again."[4]

Her new novel was also coming along. Set in rural central Florida, "The Lives of Barney Turk" followed the journey of a white Florida youth who leaves the family farm to seek high adventure in Central America. Her artistic momentum was fueled by the anticipation of her own travels and sustained in part by visits with Argentine sailors from two neighboring ships. In a letter to Burroughs Mitchell, she wrote: "I am meeting a great number of characters down here on the waterfront, and the cross section of life I am getting! It is really something."[5] Intrigued by their experiences, Hurston cast her writer's net wide and listened to their salty songs and seafaring tales as she plotted Barney's journey. But hopes for her own adventure vanished when, after months of effort, Irvine failed to attract enough cargo customers to sustain his business and was forced to put *The Challenger* up for sale.

Zora moved ashore in early January 1950, just before her fifty-ninth birthday. When her plans to buy a 57-foot schooner fell through, she spent the last of her savings to rent a studio apartment on 23rd Street in Miami. Invigorated but broke, she supported herself on loans from friends and from donations collected through local speaking engagements. She was a particular favorite at the Miami Public Library. As soon as the library's director, Frances Parsons, heard that Zora was in town, she and librarian Helga Eason made a beeline to her apartment to invite her to speak.

According to Eason, on January 23, 1950, Zora gave an utterly captivating performance at the Miami Public Library, where she shared her experiences as a folklorist and anthropologist in Jamaica, Haiti, and New Orleans. Colorfully dressed in a beautiful skirt and blouse with a matching hat, she enthralled her white audience with spine-chilling firsthand accounts of the secret practices of the voodoo religion and the belief of its followers in the supernatural.[6]

In New Orleans Hurston had studied voodoo (referred to as hoodoo in the states) under practitioner Luke Turner, the nephew of famed hoodoo priestess Marie Leveau, the city's legendary queen of conjure. While in Haiti she had risked her life; if her true purpose had been discovered—to learn the religion's secret spells, conjures, and hexes from priests known as "two-headed doctors" and become a voodoo priestess in the name of scientific research—she would not have been allowed to survive. She later exposed these secrets in vivid detail in her two collections of folklore, *Mules and Men* (1935) and *Tell My Horse* (1938).

Though Hurston's appearances were well received, the enthusiasm she generated turned to frustration when eager patrons had to wait their turn to read her books. With her works out of print except for *Seraph on the Suwanee*, the Miami Public Library had to make do with a single copy of each of her books. *Mules and Men*, a treasury of black American folklore, was by far the most popular, garnering the longest waiting list. In an effort to keep up with demand, a frustrated Eason wrote to the J. B. Lippincott Company in the hope of convincing the publisher to reprint copies of Hurston's previous books.

Lippincott had been one of Hurston's most enthusiastic supporters. When *Dust Tracks* was released in 1942, a company executive noted, "Zora Neale Hurston's books do not get the distribution they deserve, and it is up to us who are friends of hers . . . to do everything possible to spread the good word."[7] But by 1950, Lippincott had changed its tune. Much to the disappointment of Hurston and her readers, the publisher declined Eason's request, claiming that sales of her books had dwindled over the years and that it was "no longer practical" to reprint them.

While her own books on black folklore, which represented the most authentic collections to date, were no longer available, her contributions to the field were reflected in the works of others. Her former Florida Writers' Project boss Stetson Kennedy peppered his "barefoot social history of Florida," *Palmetto Country* (1942), with Zora's material. And Benjamin A. Botkin, former director of the Federal Writers' Project's Folklore Division, published two books of lore that prominently featured Hurston's work. *A Treasury of American Folklore* (1944) included twenty-one of her pieces, and *A Treasury of Southern Folklore* (1949), included nine pieces from her various works.[8] In 1950, the poet Carl Sandburg included Hurston's rendition of the song "Cold Rainy Day" in his updated collection of American songs, *New American Songbag*.[9]

Without the benefit of book sales or a steady income of any kind, Hurston was facing a financial crisis. Any royalties she would have received from *Seraph* had been applied to the $1,000 advance she had received to pay her attorney's fees. With her savings depleted, she was forced into a hand-to-mouth existence. She had hoped her speaking engagements would sustain her, but with poverty snapping at her heels, the need for reliable income could not be ignored. She had managed to complete the final draft of "Barney Turk" and was awaiting Mitchell's response. In the meantime, she accepted a temporary position as a live-in maid for the Burritt family at their exclusive Rivo Alto Island residence in Biscayne Bay. Still haunted by the shadow of scandal and embarrassed by her financial predicament, Zora never discussed her background with her employers, who in turn were never interested enough to ask. But that convenient anonymity didn't last long.

In an unexpected turn of events, Hurston was once again thrown into the national spotlight when the *Saturday Evening Post* published her short story "Conscience of the Court" in its March 1950 issue. The story, set in Jacksonville, Florida, is a courtroom drama about a loyal, lifelong black companion and servant named Laura Lee Kimble who is attacked by and then retaliates against a loan shark to prevent him from illegally removing furnishings from the home of her white mistress, Celestine Beaufort Clairborne, to collect a debt. It is a well-crafted and engaging tale that features the colorful southern folk expressions and figurative language characteristic of Hurston's style. But while the style and setting were consistent with her previous works of fiction, the characterizations contrasted sharply.

The $600 loan at the center of the story was granted to "Miz Celestine" to pay for Laura Lee's husband to be buried in Savannah, Georgia. The attack takes place after the women return from the funeral, while Celestine is in Miami. When Laura Lee sends a letter to inform her mistress of the trouble she is in, she receives no reply. Believing that she has been forsaken by a mistress to whom she has devoted her life, Laura Lee is left to face the plaintiff, the attorney, the judge, and the jury, all of whom were white, on her own. She eventually prevails after the judge, who sympathizes with her plight, demands to see a copy of the loan agreement, which proves that the loan was not due to be paid for another three months. Laura Lee also discovers that her mistress had never received the letter she had sent her.

When she is set free, feeling guilty that she had unjustly doubted "Miz Celestine's" loyalty and the justice of white folks, Laura Lee dutifully polishes the silverware to expiate her guilt before eating a meal, even though she is famished.

Given Hurston's abhorrence of racial stereotypes, her stereotypical depiction of these southern characters (reminiscent of those in Fannie Hurst's *Imitation of Life*) and their relation to each other is as ironic as it is perplexing. However, as Hemenway observes, "Any analysis of 'Conscience of the Court' is complicated by Zora's admission that the story was heavily edited by the *Post*'s staff, and by the knowledge that she badly needed to sell the story."[10]

When Mrs. Burritt read the story and the name of its author, she contacted *Miami Herald* reporter James Lyons, who quickly arranged an interview with Zora. In what was likely an effort to save face, Hurston told Lyons that she was working as a maid only to gain insight into the life of a domestic employee in preparation for a national magazine she hoped to publish by and for domestics. (She later mentioned this idea to her agent, Jean Parker Waterbury, but it never materialized.) Besides, she added, "A writer has to stop writing every now and then and just live a little."[11]

In his article, Lyons took Hurston at her word, explaining her domestic position as preparatory research and praising her as a distinguished writer, folklorist, and anthropologist. He ended the story with an optimistic quote in bold letters from Zora's philosophy of life: "If you do well today all that you are permitted to do, tomorrow you will be entrusted with something better." The article, "Famous Negro Author Working as Maid Here Just 'To Live A Little'" was published in the *Miami Herald* on March 27, 1950, and was circulated to newspapers nationally by the Associated Press. An expanded version later appeared in the *St. Louis Dispatch*.

This unexpected "slam of a publicity doo dad," as Zora phrased it, was ultimately a blessing. The flurry of media attention inspired a welcome resurgence of interest in her work and a life-affirming boost to her self-confidence. At Hurston's request, Burroughs Mitchell sent her twenty copies of *Seraph* to help keep up with local demand: "I am being lectured about at poetry & other literary clubs," she enthused. "The announcer at the Copa [Cabana Club] devoted half his time to me over the air last week."[12]

The positive publicity also brought about an offer to ghostwrite an autobiography for Judge Frank Smathers, whose son, Congressman George Smathers, was in the throes of a historic race for the U.S. Senate against the incumbent, Claude Pepper, in the Florida primary election. The judge, who had enjoyed an illustrious career, was now crippled and bedridden with rheumatoid arthritis. Only too happy to leave her domestic position, Zora accepted the offer, which included room and board as well as access to the family's extensive library, and moved into the judge's quarters, a two-bedroom apartment behind the Smathers family's home.[13]

This move put Hurston in the center of one of the most contentious and historically significant Senate campaigns in the nation's history. Senator Pepper and Congressman Smathers, both Democrats, had been political allies and friends until 1945, when their ideologies diverged on some of the same domestic and foreign issues that dominated their campaigns in 1950. Pepper was a progressive New Deal liberal who supported a U.S.-Soviet alliance, increased Social Security benefits, and a national health-care system. Smathers, a moderate and a Cold Warrior, considered Soviet aggression a dangerous threat to peace and democracy, higher Social Security payments too expensive, and a public health-care system a loss of personal freedom.

The increasing number of black voters and their demand for equality made the civil rights issue a slippery slope for southern Democratic candidates. Smathers and Pepper had to quietly court the black vote without provoking the ire of racially intolerant white voters. The fickle nature of their positions on race reflected this uneasy compromise.

During Pepper's 1944 reelection to the Senate, he had reminded voters that he had never voted for a civil rights measure and had declared that the "South will allow nothing to impair white supremacy."[14] In 1948, he had reversed his position, telling a group of Young Democrats at the University of Florida that he intended to "support President Truman's whole program of civil rights even if it beats me in the next election."[15] When his 1950 reelection campaign began, Pepper flip-flopped again and promised Florida voters that he was "absolutely opposed to any attempt by the government to abolish or interfere in any way with the customs and traditions of the Southland."[16]

Unlike Pepper, Smathers did not have to answer to a statewide constituency. The representative for Florida's Fourth Congressional District in Miami pledged that "all minorities will find me an outspoken and vigilant defender" who will "never be guilty of fanning the flames of class hatred and bigotry in order to secure votes."[17] According to biographer Brian Crispell, Smathers advocated a moderate southern approach that allowed slow progress toward racial equality. Like Hurston, he did not believe that civil rights legislation would change social mores: "I don't like bigotry and intolerance, but they do exist and I don't think you're going to get them out by passing laws."[18]

Although he supported federal intervention in defense of voting rights, he believed that all other racial matters should be left in the hands of state and local government. True to his convictions, he was largely responsible for gaining admission for black Americans to the

University of Miami football games at the Orange Bowl. His efforts also led to the improvement of black hospitals and vocational training, the establishment of a small black police force, and financial assistance for the black newspaper *Miami Times* during a wartime paper shortage.[19]

However, as a candidate for the Senate, Smathers backed away from "outspoken and vigilant" and denied his record of support for racial progress. He also played to the fears of white voters by suggesting that the Fair Employment Practices Commission, a watchdog organization created to protect workers from discriminatory employment practices, was a catalyst for communists to force desegregation on the South and promote miscegenation. "If they can pass a law to say whom you may hire and fire, they can pass one to say whom your daughter will marry," he argued.[20]

Hurston viewed the subject of civil rights legislation, arguably the most important issue of the twentieth century, with a jaundiced eye. Although she vigorously supported equality for all Americans, she considered proposals for civil rights legislation a farce that had little value other than as a clever means to attract Negro votes: "Every year, for as long as I can remember, these bills are brought up, filibustered and laid aside till next time. . . . The Northern Democrats can propose it, knowing full well that the Southerners will kill it off, then all the politicians, White and Black, can pose as great heroes, and save it for the next campaign. Why finish off something that has been good for so many Negro votes?"[21]

The way she saw it, black citizens had already been granted their rights by the U.S. Constitution, the taproot that extended and protected civil rights for all Americans. All that was actually needed, she argued, was enforcement: "All we need, all we ever needed since the passing of the Fourteenth and Fifteenth Amendments, is for the fundamental law of the land to be enforced."[22]

Hurston's writings during the period clearly demonstrate her belief that civil rights for African Americans and all minorities would not be enforced by state and local governments when public opinion was overwhelmingly against it. Her conviction was underscored by the violent response to the increasing number of black voters in the southern states, an issue she raised in a letter to *New York World* columnist Helen Worden Erskine:

> It seems to me that it all comes back to the fundamental fact that general public opinion is not quite ready as yet to accept the descendants of slaves as equals as yet , and national and state executives have not the courage as yet to buck that public opinion. In some spots in the South, Georgia, South Carolina and Mississippi, for example, it would take a lot of enforcing, as can be seen from what is going on at this moment. Honey, I see by the papers that them folks is good and *mad*![23]

Hurston believed that social justice for her race could best be won gradually, through self-reliance and self-respect acquired through cultural, intellectual, and spiritual achievement. She concluded that while African Americans were not responsible for the conditions that led to systemic inequities in American society, it was their responsibility to change them.[24] She professed, "I know that I cannot accept responsibility for thirteen million people. Every tub must sit on its own bottom regardless."[25] In other words, once her people proved themselves worthy, political, social, and economic reward would follow.

Her conclusions, though consistent with her individualist pull-yourself-up-by-your-own-boot-straps philosophy, were at odds with that of most African Americans, particularly those who had risked their lives to battle fascism abroad and were no longer willing to accept racism at home. Their resolve to challenge the Jim Crow system combined with a succession of legal victories for the NAACP, the inspiration the NAACP's leadership provided, and the thrust of President Truman's civil rights campaign created a powerful force in the face of white resistance. Black leaders in the North and South alike were sounding the clarion call for racial equality, and men like Harry T. Moore were answering it.

Moore, Florida's NAACP secretary and harbinger of hope, defied white resistance by forming the Progressive Voters League to help lead a statewide drive to register black voters. As a result of his patriotic and courageous efforts, the number of registered black Democratic voters in Florida had skyrocketed to 116,145 by the May 1950 primary, a nearly sixfold increase from 1944, the year the Supreme Court had outlawed white primaries.[26]

As the struggle for civil rights continued, Zora had her own challenges. Working for Judge Smathers was like running against the wind of a Category 5 hurricane. He had a beastly disposition, and his bigoted southern heritage made it difficult for him to accept the fact that a female "descendant of slaves" could complete an intellectual task that he could not. The judge was a brilliant but cantankerous "old cuss" who intimidated everyone except Zora. A prisoner in his own body, he developed a nasty habit of venting his frustration over his debilitating physical condition by goading his family members into arguments and making wild accusations and then refusing to allow anyone to respond to them. While his family felt obligated to indulge him, Zora adamantly refused.

In a letter to Mitchell, a defiant Hurston declared, "I do not beat down easily, and we fought like tigers from day to day, and I came to see that he loved it. He had met at last a foeman worthy of his steel."[27] Judge Smathers was to realize in a few short months what it took most segregationists a lifetime to discern—the absolute absurdity of racism. The experience of matching wits with Zora, known during the Harlem Renaissance as "Queen of the Niggerati," was the most powerful argument against it. When the judge refused to hear her side of an argument by plugging his ears with his fingers, Hurston informed him that he would listen to her, simply pulled his fingers out, and went on talking.

Zora's behavior toward the irascible judge sometimes offended his wife Lura, but it amused and delighted his sons George and Frank junior, who thought she was simply magnificent. Beneath his tough exterior, Judge Smathers unquestionably agreed. When his wife objected to Zora's tongue-lashing him, he staunchly defended her and insisted that she was welcome to remain with them forever if she liked.[28]

Hurston's ability to match wits with the judge was reason enough for veneration, but George Smathers and his wife Rosemary also admired her for her uncommon talent and intellect. In addition to a strong mutual regard, Hurston and Smathers shared similar social and political views, including a staunch anti-communist stance, opposition to the racially charged Federal Employment Practices Commission, and a mistrust of labor unions. During the election she actively campaigned for him, telling voters that his opponent may be spicy to listen to, but "You can't make a meal off of Pepper."[29]

Hurston's support for Smathers's candidacy over the more "liberal" Pepper has created a conundrum for even her most ardent defenders. However, while her views were sometimes abstruse and always complicated, her political alliance with Smathers was consistent with the prevailing view of the majority of the country, including that of President Truman. Hurston was appalled by Pepper's pandering to white supremacists and his positive view of communist Russia.

During World War II, the majority of Americans had hoped that Russia and America would remain friends and allies. Claude Pepper, an internationalist and a senior member of the Senate Foreign Relations Committee, was among those who shared this view. A few weeks after the war ended, Pepper set out on a goodwill tour of several major European countries, including Russia. After a short meeting with Stalin, Pepper praised the leader in an address on Russian radio, calling him "one of the great men of history and the world."[30] Upon his return to the United States, Pepper told the *New York Times* that he felt "privileged to talk with the single most powerful man in the world, the man who is going to determine in a large way what kind of world ours is to be."[31] Pepper's statements reflected his sincere, though naive, belief that Russia would continue to back the U.S. postwar peacekeeping mission.

Pepper's good intentions were misunderstood back home. His praise of Stalin offended many Americans who believed that Truman, not Stalin, was the single most powerful man in the world. After returning from Russia, the *Fort Lauderdale News* reported that "Claude Pepper believes in Communism. WE DO NOT. That's why we suggest that the sooner you realize he is NOT a part of OUR AMERICAN WAY OF LIFE the better off we will be."[32] The negative press was only part of the backlash. His trip abroad also infuriated some of his constituents, who felt that his travels were unnecessary expenditures of energy and time that would have been better spent solving the problems in his home state. Although Pepper refused to admit it, his support for Stalin was the worst political mistake of his career.

By 1946, Stalin's refusal to end the Soviet occupation of Eastern Europe had launched the Cold War. The American shift in attitude toward the Soviets created a serious ideological and political problem for Pepper. His miscalculation of Stalin's intentions infuriated President Truman, alienated Florida voters, generated negative press, and sparked an investigation of his affiliations by the FBI.[33]

Smathers was a shrewd politician who knew how to play on his opponent's weakness and saw Pepper's support for Stalin as his Achilles' heel. Smathers unfairly flagged Pepper as a communist sympathizer, which later set him up for comparisons with the ill-fated and mentally unstable Senator Joe McCarthy, who used the fear of communism to gain political advantage. But unlike McCarthy, who pulled his accusations out of thin air, Smathers used Pepper's own words and actions to bait the trap. When Winston Churchill warned the United States of the dangers of Soviet aggression in his "Iron Curtain" speech, Pepper criticized him, accusing the United States and Britain of "ganging up" against Russia. In a speech on April 4, 1946, entitled "Peace through Justice for All Nations," Pepper called America the "guarantor of British imperialism," implying that Britain's imperialism posed more of a threat than the Soviet Union.

In response, the *Washington Post* printed an editorial entitled "Red Pepper" that warned, "If he [Pepper] keeps it up, he will be making a strong bid for the distinction of being America's number one whitewasher of aggression."[34] This criticism by the press continued throughout the 1950 campaign and largely contributed to Pepper's defeat. By the May primary, all but two major Florida newspapers had endorsed Smathers.

By the time Zora moved into the Smathers' household in April, the Senate race had become an all-out slugfest and the most closely watched campaign in the nation. The *Miami Herald* assigned reporters to both candidates to record every colorful quip, phrase, and accusation the candidates uttered.[35] Ironically, of all the controversial statements Smathers made during the campaign, he is best remembered (and most frequently quoted) for a speech that he never made that is often referred to as the "celibacy" or "thespian" speech.

The infamous speech was supposed to have been delivered to the poor "backwoods" residents of North Florida to take advantage of their limited vocabulary. Smathers was quoted as saying: "Are you aware that Claude Pepper is known all over Washington as a shameless extrovert? Not only that, but this man is reliably reported to practice nepotism with his sister-in-law and he has a sister who was once a thespian in wicked New York. Worst of all, it is an established fact that Mr. Pepper, before his marriage, habitually practiced celibacy."[36]

For Smathers to have insulted the intelligence of his audience would not only have been the height of stupidity, it would have been political suicide. Even in the backwoods of northern Florida there were educators, attorneys, and businessmen. The controversy over the lines dogged Smathers throughout his career, until finally in 1965 he offered a $10,000 reward to anyone who could prove that he made that speech. No one came forward.[37]

Hurston and Pepper were also at odds about labor unions. While Pepper supported them, Hurston did not trust labor unions. She believed they were communist-backed organizations that made empty promises to blacks in return for their votes and took a public stand when vote-selling became a major issue in the campaign. The controversy began when Democratic Party chairman Jerry Carter asked the Congress of Industrial Organizations (CIO) to come to Florida and assist him in his efforts to deliver the vote for Pepper. In response to the request, the CIO's Political Action Committee (PAC) sent a black official, Philip Weightman, to Florida to organize voter registration drives in Jacksonville, Tampa, and Miami.

Their registration efforts were stymied when Florida newspapers reported stories of CIO/PAC operatives giving free groceries, movie tickets, and money to blacks who registered to vote. In late March, the *Miami Herald* reported that "in some areas, registration clerks were quoted to the effect that most Negroes were coming in to register in the company of the same four or five Negro men, and one courthouse report had the recruiters getting twenty-five cents a head."[38]

Hurston responded to the reports by completing her own investigation, which formed the basis of her essay, "I Saw Negro Votes Peddled," published first in *Negro Digest* on September 9, 1950, and reprinted in the *American Legion Magazine* in November of the same year. In this biting political commentary, she accused the CIO of corrupting the black vote by promoting a "voting for what-you-could-get" mania and perpetuating the systematic exploitation of blacks by depriving them of the ability to vote their conscience.

When the poll sites opened in Miami for the primary, Hurston drove from one black precinct to another, observing and talking to participants. By the end of the day, she was convinced that black voters were being paid $2 a head to "single-shot" vote by pulling a single lever (presumably for Pepper) and ignoring everything else on the ballot, but the CIO denied it. One poll worker told Zora, "These are poor working people, and we are giving them two dollars apiece to pay them for their time to take off long enough from their jobs to cast their vote."[39]

Regardless of how the union viewed it, Zora was bristling with righteous indignation. Taking aim at black voters who she believed had been willing to sell "the most potent weapon in a republic" for a cheap price, she complained: "There have been more public debates, more preachments, more laws proposed and passed, more contention, and yes, more human bloodshed, to bring us to the place where we can cast our ballot . . . than anybody else in America. . . . It is positively astounding that any adult Negro could look upon the right to vote as a small thing, let alone regard this highest right in civilization in such a way as to put a price upon it."[40]

Hurston's admonishments, though well intended, provoked strong criticism. Lester Granger of the Urban League took umbrage at her characterization of black voters as "childishly gullible." And Bill Baggs, the white editor of *Miami News*, publicly challenged Hurston's accusations of vote-selling: "I have spent considerable time and effort trying to confirm the charges she has made, and I cannot turn up anything more than hearsay."[41] Baggs suggested that if Zora's assertions were correct, somebody should be prosecuted. And if they were not, he insisted that "Miss Hurston should be revealed as a purveyor of raw sensationalism, who will go to the limit to make a buck."[42]

When the primary election was held in May, George Smathers was victorious over Claude Pepper, earning 55 percent of the vote. He then easily defeated his Republican opponent, Stetson Kennedy, in the November 1950 general election and served in the U.S. Senate until 1969. (Claude Pepper returned to Congress in 1963 where, among other issues, he distinguished himself as a champion for the rights of the elderly, working tirelessly to strengthen the Social Security program.) No longer distracted by the hurly-burly of the campaign, Zora shifted her attention to the work of an old friend, Sara Creech, whose doll project would capture the hearts and minds of thousands of America's children.

3

SARA CREECH AND
HER BEAUTIFUL DOLL

Belle Glade, 1950–1951

*The thing that pleased me most . . . was that you, a White
girl, should have seen into our hearts so clearly, and sought
to meet our longing for understanding of us as we really are,
and not as some would have us. That you have not insulted
us by a grotesque caricature of Negro children, but conceived
something of real Negro beauty.*

After the election, Hurston continued to ghostwrite for Judge
Smathers. In early May, at the request of her friend Sara Creech, she
drove over 120 miles to Belle Glade, Florida, the little farming community that had inspired the setting in *Their Eyes Were Watching God*. The
purpose of her visit was to speak to the members of the innovative
Belle Glade Inter-Racial Council. Comprised of fifteen white and fifteen black members, the council had been founded in 1948 by Creech
and other socially enlightened residents in response to the region's
deepening racial discord. In the summer of 1943, racial tensions in
Dixie had set off some of the worst violence since the notorious long
bloody summer of 1919, when race riots and lynch mobs had swept
the South like a tidal wave. In an effort to promote racial harmony,
members of the council met monthly to identify the needs of Belle
Glade's black and migrant communities and devise the means to address them.

Zora's public appearances were always extraordinary, and her
first speaking engagement at the council's May 7, 1950, meeting was

nothing less than that. Creech recalled, "She came dressed in a lovely white linen dress and was every bit the Barnard scholar."[1] But as memorable as that appearance was, Creech insisted that Zora's encore performance several years later was a tour de force. On that occasion a gloriously flamboyant Zora walked onto the stage of the Lake Shore School auditorium draped in a sultry, full-length, fiery red sheath and matching red turban and dazzled the standing-room-only crowd: "For a solid hour she moved in and out of dialects as she recited folk tales, sang work songs, and danced. Before she left the stage, the windows outside the building were lined with onlookers caught up in her spell."[2]

Hurston was every bit as impressed with the council as it was with her. It was the second organization of its kind in the state (the other was in Orlando) and a shining example of racial cooperation for the public good. Soon after her May 7 visit, she wrote a congratulatory letter commending Creech for the role she had played in its founding:

> I suppose that I should not be surprised by the steps you have taken, for never was I more surprised and delighted than when I spoke at Belle Glade and found your extraordinary inter-racial organization. It could be a model for the nation, and according to what I hear, you, Sara Creech are at the very heart of it. This follows a conclusion that I reached some years ago from observation. That is, that the so-called Race Problem will be solved in the South and by Southerners. I have noted that when a Southerner becomes convinced, he goes all out for correcting the situation.[3]

Creech, who had known Zora for several years, was the embodiment of Hurston's unshakable belief that individuals, not groups, were the point of origin for social and political change. In addition to her work on the council, the redheaded, sixth-generation white southerner had established an award-winning preschool, Wee Care, for the children of migrant workers and was working toward the creation of a quality "anthropologically correct" black doll.

The idea for the doll sprang from an epiphany following a conversation she'd had around Christmas in 1949 with Louise Taylor, a black mother, who complained that the only quality dolls available for her daughters were white. A few days later, Creech noticed two black girls playing with white dolls and was struck by the contrast. Convinced that black children needed and deserved a doll that would reflect the physical beauty of their own race, she decided to look into the matter. In the months that followed, her query became a mission, which a *People Today* reporter deemed "the most laborious toy project in history."[4]

As a result of her research, Creech discovered that the only African American dolls being produced in the United States at that time were predominately pickaninny rag dolls, handkerchief-headed servant dolls, and grotesque Negro caricatures. One of the few affordable alternatives to these degrading stereotypes were cheaply made Caucasian dolls that were painted brown.[5]

The idea of painting white dolls brown and passing them off as African American was introduced by the P & M Doll Company in 1919 with the production of its Daisy doll. This doll, which sold for $1.95, was made of cheap plastic and was often a factory reject that had been recycled and painted. A few years later P & M created a black Topsy doll, named after a character in Harriet Beecher Stowe's *Uncle Tom's Cabin*. The new doll sold well to white customers but was shunned by African Americans and widely condemned for its racially charged banjo eyes and the pickaninny braids sprouting from the top of its head. Nevertheless, both dolls remained popular with white consumers well into the 1950s.[6]

It wasn't until the late 1940s that several pioneering companies produced black dolls based on popular fictional characters as alternatives to the stereotypical and faux black dolls that dominated the market. In 1947, the Terri Lee Corporation created Patty-Jo, a light-skinned teenaged black doll, modeled after a popular cartoon character created by black artist Jackie Ormes for the *Pittsburgh Courier*. Patty-Jo was a beautifully crafted doll costumed in expensive cowgirl clothes, boots, and hat. However, few stores in the South carried the doll, and where it was available, its $15.95 price tag ($153 in 2010 dollars) put it out of reach for most families.[7]

That same year, the ten-inch plastic baby Amosandra doll, which sold for $2.98, made its debut. Amosandra, touted by Macy's as "The Sweetest Doll In Town," was released on Valentine's Day, one week after the fictitious birth of a baby with the same name to radio characters Andy and Ruby Jones on the *Amos 'n' Andy Show*. According to *Ebony* magazine, in spite of a "crippling" snowstorm, Macy's department store in New York City sold 400 dolls in the first two days, mostly to white patrons.[8]

While these worthy efforts advanced the idea of creating realistic Negro dolls, the disturbing fact remained that no American toy maker had yet produced a quality doll with authentic African American features. The closest any company had come was in 1950 when the Allied Grand Company introduced its Jackie Robinson doll in honor of the famed baseball star.[9]

Appalled by this racial slight, Creech decided it was time to rescue black children from further humiliation. Her convictions were bolstered by the pioneering research conducted in 1939 by sociologists Kenneth and Mamie Clark to determine the degree to which black children perceived racial bias. In their famous study, which was later used in the Supreme Court's groundbreaking decision in *Brown v. Board of Education of Topeka* (1954), the Clarks asked children a series of questions relating to race and observed their reactions to identical brown and white dolls. Their findings showed that the majority of African American children rejected the brown doll in preference for the white and that black children as young as three years old "suffered from self-rejection" as a result of the "corrosive awareness of color."[10]

Hurston's own orientation to the aesthetic burdens of skin color had begun at an early age. Her first encounter with color bias had come not from a racist white society but from her all-black home village of Eatonville. Although race pride was central to the community, there was a distinctive color hierarchy among its members that crippled the souls of the darker-skinned. Zora had perceived this paradox as a young child and struggled for understanding. "If it was so honorable and glorious to be black, why was it the yellow-skinned people among us had so much prestige?"[11] Even in her all-black grammar school, it was the "light-skinned children who were always the angels, fairies, and queens of school plays," she observed.[12]

Hurston alluded to this tendency of light-skinned blacks to "class off" from their darker brothers most notably in her characterization of Mrs. Turner in *Their Eyes Were Watching God*: "Ah can't stand black niggers. Ah don't blame de white folks from hatin' 'em 'cause Ah can't stand 'em mahself. . . . Dey laughs too much and dey laughs too loud. Always singin' ol' nigger songs. . . . If it wuzn't for so many black folks it wouldn't be no race problem. De white folks would take us wid dem. De black ones is holdin' us back."[13]

The tyranny of color consciousness has resonated throughout African American literature since *Clotel*, the first novel by a black American, was published in 1853.[14] Written by William Wells Brown, *Clotel*, a fanciful story about the beautiful mulatto daughter of Thomas Jefferson, takes color prejudice among the black community as its central theme. In Wallace Thurman's 1929 novel *The Blacker the Berry*, the heroine washes her face in peroxide before dashing out to a dance in Harlem. And in 1970, Toni Morrison's first novel, *The Bluest Eye*, illuminated the pressure blacks feel to live up to the beauty standards of white society. But, as one critic notes, "There is no more disconcertingly morbid document of this phenomenon than Hurston's prize-winning 'Color Struck.'"[15] Published in *Opportunity* magazine during the Harlem Renaissance, the play chronicles the life of a talented but very dark-skinned woman whose surreal descent into utter madness comes from her belief that no man could love a woman with skin like hers.

When Creech told Hurston about the doll project, she urged her, "Go ahead with it Sara, but don't go ringin' no backin' bells [a folk expression meaning "never retreat"]. Faith ain't got no eyes, but she's long-legged."[16] Taking this encouragement to heart, Creech enlisted the help of her friend Maxeda von Hesse, a human relations consultant and speech coach in New York City. Von Hesse then contacted sculptress Sheila Burlingame, who agreed to design and produce plaster castings of the doll's head and facial features.

To ensure racial authenticity, Creech took pictures of hundreds of Belle Glade children and sent them to Burlingame to use as models. When the castings were completed, Creech photographed them and sent a copy to Hurston, who lauded her efforts with heartfelt praise:

> Please allow me to say how pleased I am that you let me see pictures of the Negro dolls that you plan to put on the market. . . . The thing that pleased me most . . . was that you, a White girl, should have seen into our hearts so clearly, and sought to meet our longing for understanding of us as we really are, and not as some would have us. That you have not insulted us by a grotesque caricature of Negro children, but conceived something of real Negro beauty. Those dolls are adorable. . . . They will surely meet a long-felt need among us. It [is] a magnificently constructive thing you are doing for the whole of America as well as for Negro children.[17]

After seeing the photos, Hurston suggested a name for the doll, Saralee, after its creator, and advised Creech to show the models to "well-known and influential Negroes" who could help the project along.[18]

To aid in the effort, she provided Creech with letters of introduction to some of her most illustrious friends and acquaintances, including Fisk University president Charles S. Johnson, the former editor of *Opportunity* magazine and a guiding force of the Harlem Renaissance. Zora also wrote letters to Morehouse College president Benjamin Mays, Bethune-Cookman College founder Mary McLeod Bethune, Morris Brown College president Bishop R. R. Wright, President Mordecai Johnson of Howard University, President Rufus Clement of Atlanta University, and Washington, D.C., poet Georgia Douglas Johnson, whom she had met during her Howard University years.[19]

With letters in hand, Creech spent the summer traveling the country to meet with Hurston's power team, who welcomed the project with overwhelming enthusiasm. Bishop R. R. Wright, who had waged an unsuccessful 50-year struggle to promote the production of a quality black doll, was deeply impressed with Creech's efforts. The prototypes made an equally good impression on Dr. Benjamin Mays, who later wrote a letter of endorsement to General Robert Wood, chief executive officer of Sears, Roebuck and Co., to emphasize the doll's significance. In an encouraging letter to Creech, Mays underscored not only the doll's potential for profit but its sociological benefits as well: "I feel that a good bit of good will and human understanding can be promoted if you can get the right type of dolls manufactured that would portray the Negro child in the proper light. . . . It is the things that we learn unconsciously that will determine the extent of our prejudices towards others and the extent of our understanding."[20]

Charles S. Johnson also threw his considerable influence behind the project, as did Georgia Douglas Johnson, who called the doll a "little ambassador of peace." Rufus Clement put Creech in touch with Helen Whiting, a professor of early childhood education at Atlanta University, who raised a crucial point about the doll's color. To avoid what might otherwise be criticized as stereotypical, the doll's color had to be carefully chosen. This issue would present Creech with her greatest challenge.

While Creech pressed ahead, Hurston pursued her own projects. In June, she contacted Ed Koch, chairman of the University of Miami drama department, to propose joining forces with musicologist Alan Lomax and Carl Sandburg to produce a folk festival at Miami Stadium in the fall. When those plans fell through, Hurston fled from her ghostwriting job for Judge Smathers, telling Mitchell: "I wanted the money, but never did I think I was taking on such a task."[21] The strain of living with and attending to the judge left her emotionally drained and longing for solitude. "Oh to be once more alone in a house!" she later wrote her agent, Jean Parker Waterbury.[22] But first there were more pressing matters to attend to.

After moving into the Miami home of friends Samuel and Evelyn Gomez, she worked at white heat to complete her editor's suggested revisions on her latest novel. "Getting along fast and well on the new 'Barney Turk.' I am glad now that I am doing it over. You will have it in your hands much sooner than you think," she assured Mitchell.[23]

In September, when the revisions were complete, a hopeful Hurston headed to New York to personally deliver the manuscript to Scribner's and to be on site for the final editing.

Zora's return to the Big Apple was enthusiastically embraced by Carl Van Vechten, who announced to a mutual friend, "Zora in person is in town!"[24] After settling into a room on Harlem's West 131st Street, Zora began socializing with her old circle of friends for the first time since the scandal. On October 29 she likely attended a dinner, along with guest speaker Van Vechten, to honor the outstanding achievements of their friend Ethel Waters, who was starring on Broadway in Carson McCullers's *The Member of the Wedding*. Known for a smile that could melt an iceberg, Waters was the first black actress to receive star billing on Broadway and in movies.

Hurston also paid several visits to Sara Creech, who had come to New York at the invitation of former first lady Eleanor Roosevelt to discuss the promotion of her Saralee doll. After meeting with the first lady at her Val-Kill Cottage, Creech scheduled a meeting with United Nations director of trusteeship Dr. Ralph Bunche, recipient of the 1950 Nobel Peace Prize, and sociologist David Rosenstein, president of Ideal Toy Company, to seek support for the doll's production. During her stay, Creech was a guest at 36 Sutton Place, the home of her friend Maxeda von Hesse and her mother Elizabeth, Mrs. Roosevelt's personal speech coach.

"Zora took a shine to Maxeda from the moment I introduced them," Creech recalled.[25] In addition to her speaking credentials, the 34-year-old von Hesse was a humanist, an author, a lecturer, and an unpublished playwright. During the early years of her career, von Hesse had worked as a nonfiction staff writer for the *American Magazine* and as a director and producer for the National Broadcasting Corporation. After completing graduate studies at Northwestern University, she became director of her mother's speech studios in New York, the Von Hesse Studios of Effective Speech and Human Relations.[26] Zora admired Maxeda's writing ability and even shared and discussed some of her own work with her.[27]

Creech described Zora's visits to Sutton Place as warm and lively. Although she had been critical of FDR's New Deal—which she believed had whipped up "racial antagonism" and encouraged sympathy for communism—Zora admired Eleanor Roosevelt and took particular pleasure in hearing about the Von Hesses' personal and professional experiences at the Roosevelt White House. They, in turn, were fascinated by Zora's life and work. "Zora charmed the Von Hesses with her wit, talent, and humor in the same way that she charmed everyone else who met her," Creech enthused. "They were quite taken with her brilliant mind and effervescent personality."[28]

As the doll's official godmother, Hurston's visits to Sutton Place included personal updates on Saralee. Her letters of introduction had played a vital role in the doll's manufacture, and she continued to promote it with characteristic zeal among her Harlem friends. One such friend, Carl Van Vechten, became one of the doll's most ardent supporters and later used his considerable clout to secure a full spread on the doll's debut in the December 1951 issue of *Life* magazine.[29]

In addition to their hopes for the doll's success, Creech and von Hesse shared an enthusiasm for what Hurston hoped would be another cultural milestone, the first "truly indigenous Negro novel" ever written. Her manuscript, later titled "The Golden Bench of God," was based on the true-life rags-to-riches story of one of the country's first black female millionaires, Madame C. J. Walker, and her daughter A'Lelia. In the early 1900s, the elder Walker had built an empire with her hair-care products and hair-straightening technique for black women. A'Lelia Walker, famous for her bohemian Harlem parties, had been an acquaintance of Zora in the 1920s. Hurston had been encouraged by Jean Parker Waterbury and a script man at the Robert Whitehead Theatrical Agency to write the story as a novelette with the hope that it would follow the same course as Carson McCullers's popular novelette-turned-play *The Member of the Wedding*.

Unlike her short story "Conscience of the Court," which had been written to a formula intended to sell, "The Golden Bench of God" was inspired by Hurston's unyielding desire to present a view of black life unpoisoned by racial strife. Throughout her career, she fought for the freedom to write what she wanted, and she had always desired to present an authentic depiction of African Americans that showcased their cultural, ideological, and esthetic significance. In an interview for the *Amsterdam News*, Zora once told a reporter that a black writer's "material is controlled by publishers who think of the Negro as picturesque."[30]

Hurston's novels about the "folks farthest down" had been commercially successful, but the prevailing view of her white publisher was that a predominately white readership had no interest in the lives of bourgeois or middle-class minorities. In 1945, when Hurston submitted a story idea about the upper strata of Negro life titled "Mrs. Doctor," her editors turned it down. Undaunted by previous failure, the celebrant of black culture was compelled to try again: "Punches have been pulled to 'keep things from the white folks' or angled politically, well to show our suffering, rather than to tell a story as is," Hurston told Jean Parker Waterbury.[31] "I have decided that the time has come to write truthfully from the inside. Imagine that no white audience is present to hear what is said."[32]

As a writer who had long struggled to achieve a balance between artistic freedom and commercial success, Zora was keenly aware of the publishing industry's need for profit. However, as an anthropologist and cultural relativist, she also recognized the social and cultural consequences of the restrictions imposed on black writers by a racist American society. As biographer Robert Hemenway noted, "Even such a brilliant poet as Gwendolyn Brooks has been advised that if 'being a Negro' is her only subject, then she is somehow prohibited from creating great literature."[33]

Zora took aim at this cultural blockade in her now-famous satirical essay, "What White Publishers Won't Print." Published in *Negro Digest* in April 1950, Hurston warned her readers that the lack of interest of Anglo-Saxons in "the internal lives and emotions of the Negroes, and for that matter, any non-Anglo-Saxon peoples . . . above the class of unskilled labor" only fostered ignorance and racial intolerance. With a seasoned pen and a genius for metaphor, she argued that white antipathy toward minority races in American society had perpetuated racial stereotypes and created a "Museum of Unnatural History." In this museum of cultural myths, the American Indian is presented as a stoic figure "in an eternal war-bonnet, with no equipment for laughter" and the Negro as a mechanical toy with "shuffling feet and rolling eyes." In the last paragraph, she challenged publishers and filmmakers alike to muster the courage to change these ridiculous perceptions: "Let there be light!"[34]

While Hurston's enthusiasm for her novelette grew, her hopes for "Barney" sank after a year of toil and sacrifice when Scribner's declined to publish it. In a letter dated October 3, 1950, an apologetic Mitchell explained that although her manuscript showcased "wonderful flashes of writing," the story lacked the power to hold the reader's attention.[35] He felt that it would damage her professional standing to publish a novel that lacked the stylistic breadth of her previous work. Apparently, "The Lives of Barney Turk" lacked the characteristic passion and affection that Zora had so abundantly bestowed upon the characters in her novels about rural folk life. Or, as biographer Valerie Boyd aptly phrased it, "the absence of love was palpable on the page."[36] In a sincere effort to assuage her disappointment and point her in a potentially more profitable direction, Mitchell suggested that Hurston put fiction aside temporarily and work on the second volume of her autobiography. But Zora had little interest in writing another book on her life, preferring instead to continue working on her novelette.

In November, she attended a cocktail party at Van Vechten's home and continued her visits with Creech and von Hesse. While she enjoyed the social interaction, Zora's fall arrival had stretched well into winter, and she disliked being trapped in the New York winter of "bare trees, cold winds, dirty snow under foot, no birds, no blooms."[37] Her return to Harlem had also stirred painful memories of the false molestation charges, which further darkened her mood. Just before Christmas, in a letter to Charles S. Johnson, Hurston railed against her black intellectual detractors, including Richard Wright and W. E. B. Dubois, who had been associated with the Communist Party, and brazenly suggested that they may have played a role in the false moral charges: "Because I openly expressed my scorn of them, they got up what they took to be an unbeatably wonderful scheme to kill me off forever. Only these monumental 'intellectuals,' in their ecstasy, did not take the time to find out where I was when they stated the dates for things."[38]

A few weeks before Christmas 1950, having no further business in New York, Hurston began making plans to return to Florida. As Creech recalled, she had easily convinced Zora to move to Belle Glade, but when she suggested they make the long drive home together, Hurston refused. "It was a matter of practicality and safety," Creech explained. "Zora was concerned about the problems we would face as traveling companions. Since hotels and motels were segregated, she knew it would have been impossible for us to find lodging together."[39]

In an effort to avoid any racial complications, at Hurston's insistence, Creech booked a flight to Florida and Zora made her own way home. After a short visit with her brother John in Jacksonville, Zora arrived in Belle Glade in late December at the height of cane-burning season, when the dead leaves around the cane stalks are burned away to make processing easier. The spectacular view of red and yellow flames in every direction make it look as though the horizon itself is ablaze. Creech had invited Zora to live with her and her mother Mary, but preferring a more private living arrangement, she rented a room at the Roof Garden Hotel. Located on the outskirts of the city's black business community and named for the lush garden on its rooftop, the Roof Garden was an attractive two-story cement building surrounded by a scattering of houses and small neighboring farms. Her single room had neither cooking facilities nor a private bathroom, but it was conveniently located only a few miles from Creech's home and the sandy white shores of Lake Okeechobee.[40]

When Hurston had visited Belle Glade to collect folklore in 1927, it had been an unincorporated frontier with a few farms, two stores, a gas station, and a hotel. By 1950 it had grown into a thriving agricultural mecca with a significant black workforce. The streets of the small stop-at-the-stop-sign-and-wave black community were lined with an eclectic assortment of locally owned businesses and restaurants where the smells of home-style cookin' wafted out to tempt the pass-erby. Informal gatherings were held at Maynor's Hair Salon and Houston's Drugstore, where the gossip went out as fast as it came in.[41] On the weekends, the sweet rounded notes of the blues floated from The Clubhouse on Main Street, and the jook joints were still jumpin' just like Tea Cake had described them in *Their Eyes Were Watching God*: "All night now the jooks clanged and clamored. Pianos living three life-times in one. Blues made and used right on the spot. Dancing, fighting, singing, crying, laughing, winning and losing love every hour."[42]

After settling into her small room, Zora adopted a black-and-white terrier and named her Spot. "She adored the dog and took her ev-erywhere she went. She was a smart dog with a sweet disposition," Creech recalled.[43] Zora's attachment was so strong that she was in-consolable when the dog went missing in February 1951. Fortunately, Spot returned to Zora's care after a two-week hiatus, a little thinner and pregnant but no worse for the wear.

Christine Maynor, owner of Maynor's Hair Salon, described Zora as friendly but private. In addition to the hair salon, Maynor also owned a small ice cream parlor located close to the Roof Garden Hotel. "I met Zora for the first time when she dropped by for some ice cream," Maynor recalled.[44] "After introducing herself, she said she was a writer and asked me if I had a dictionary she could borrow. I didn't have a dictionary at the shop, but I brought one from home and gave it to her the next time I saw her. She didn't say much about herself, but she oc-casionally sat in on the local gossiping sessions in front of Houston's Drug Store. She also liked to tell stories to the local children who gath-ered in front of her hotel."[45]

Hurston spent most of her time and energy writing her novelette "The Golden Bench of God" and researching the life of the ancient Judean ruler King Herod the Great, the intended subject of her next play. On her lazy days, she'd cast a cane pole in mighty Lake Okeecho-bee or, when the fish weren't biting, head south in her car to explore the magnificent sweep of the Florida Everglades. She was particularly fond of visiting the Seminole Indian Reservation, where she had made friends with Sally Tiger-Tail, daughter of Chief Billy Cyprus, who gave her gifts of authentic Seminole clothing.[46] She also attended Belle Glade Inter-Racial Council meetings and spent a considerable amount of time with the Creech family, for whom she had developed a great deal of affection.

Zora's admiration for Sara and her mother was evident in her correspondence with writer Carl Sandburg. In a letter to the poet, Hurston introduced Creech as "perhaps the foremost individual of the area for better race relations" and dubbed her "a white phenomenon" who brought about change with a velvet hammer: "Talented and balanced, she does force in such a quiet way that she moves things."[47]

It is easy to see how Hurston could have formed such a deep connection with these women. Both Sara and Mary Creech were fiercely independent, strong-willed, highly intelligent, and deeply compassionate individuals who embraced Hurston's friendship with their hearts, minds, and souls. And having been close to a mother with the same characteristics, Zora must have found a comfort and familiarity with them that felt like home.

In addition to her community leadership, 34-year-old Sara was an astute business woman who, like Zora, found marriage too constrictive and ended her first and only attempt after less than a year. Mary Creech, whom Hurston described as "extraordinary," was a devoted mother who instilled in her children a strong sense of morality as well as the virtues of a good book, often reminding them "You'll never be alone with a poet in your pocket."[48]

Sara, a native of Sparta, Georgia, had moved to Belle Glade in 1934 to live with her brother Bob, who owned a farm on nearby Ritta Island. After graduating from high school, she started an insurance agency forty-five miles to the east in Lake Worth. When her father died in 1941, she moved back to Belle Glade with her mother, built a house on Canal Street, opened the city's first florist shop, and became a permanent "muckstepper," the name given to those who live on the "muck," the coal-black organic soil that covers the Glades. Seventy-six-year-old Mary operated the florist shop from a large room on the side of their home, and in 1951 Creech opened an insurance agency in town.

Zora and Spot would often walk down 5th Street to Creech's house after breakfast and stay all day. While Sara tended to business, Zora and Mary worked in the flower shop or spent the day in the family library wrapped in a cloud of companionship. Their lively and candid pondering, which often continued for hours, would invariably sail off in all directions. "Zora didn't shock us," Creech declared. "We didn't always agree with her, but we were well-accustomed to her controversial opinions."[49]

Having developed friendships with numerous whites throughout her life, Hurston was comfortable with them and would often sympathize with them. During one of their conversations, she boldly told Mary Creech that "Lincoln probably did more for the poor whites of the South by Emancipation, than he did for us. . . . When you think of the generations of individual talent among the poor whites that never got a hearing, it is truly tragic."[50]

In preparation for her King Herod script, Zora spent many hours in the Creech family library engaged in research on Jewish and Christian history. In her rather erudite, velvet-soft drawl, Creech recalled that "on the days I was around, I remember mother [she pronounced it 'muh thuh'] and Zora reading and discussing Josephus's history and passages from the Bible in great detail."[51] Afterward, she would stay for dinner, which she often cooked. "You knew you were in for a sumptuous Southern meal when Zora was in the kitchen," Creech declared.[52] A typical Hurston feast included fried chicken or the fish she had caught that day, turnip greens (flavored with ham hocks), mashed potatoes, and, for desert, a custard-like dish called sweet-potato pone. "There's an art to making good potato pone," Creech enthused. "But that wasn't hard for Zora; she was an excellent cook."[53]

Sara described 60-year-old Hurston as "proud, self-confident, optimistic, hardworking, and playful."[54] She recalled, "Zora had lived through some very difficult circumstances in her life, yet you would have never known it by her demeanor."[55] Her casual conversation, which was punctuated by southern idiom, was often laced with laughter and spiced with wit. She had been critically neglected, artistically stifled, and professionally limited by her gender and race, and the years and circumstances had left their marks. But for all she had suffered, Hurston adamantly and consistently refused to be defined or measured by the yardstick of others.

Proud and determined, she wrote various articles and a book review to support herself. In January 1951, she began an article for the *American Legion* magazine and wrote a review of Philippe Thoby Marcelin's novel *Pencil of God* for the *New York Tribune*. The *Legion*, which had reprinted a copy of her previously published essay on the political exploitation of black voters, "I Saw Votes Peddled," had offered her $600 to write an article on the Communist Party's exploitation of the Negro. Over the years, she had made no secret of her abhorrence of communism, a hatred that had taken hold in the late 1920s when friend and poet Langston Hughes had taken an interest in it. In her article "Why Negroes Won't Buy Communism," published in the magazine's June 1951 issue, Hurston argued that African Americans were neither impressed nor persuaded by the Communist Party's "patronizing" recruitment efforts. Her assertion was that they resented the party's characterization of them as "pitiable" and rejected its way of life, which was "as morbid and ugly as the devil's doll-baby."

As Carla Kaplan observes, Hurston's anti-communist stance "was not fundamentally askew of the view held by many other black anti-communists writing during this period."[56] In fact, according to African American historian Wilson Record, from the 1940s "few criticisms of the Communist Party in this country, from whatever source, have equaled the NAACP's."[57] Kaplan states that the organization adopted a policy prohibiting communists from joining the association in 1950.[58] To emphasize the point, NAACP acting secretary Roy Wilkins sent a memo to national branches to remind members of the organization's determination to "condemn and actively oppose . . . attempts of various groups, particularly Communists, either to secure control of our branches outright, or to use the branches as sounding boards for political and other ideas."[59]

In addition to her article opposing communism, Zora also made a pitch to her agent Jean Parker Waterbury about an article on the lives of sugar-cane cutters who had been recruited from the West Indies.

Sugar cane, primarily grown on the south end of Lake Okeechobee, was first grown with significant commercial success by United States Sugar Corporation in 1931. Over the eleven years that followed, the company's recruiters traveled to cities throughout the South to find laborers to hand-cut the cane. Their practice was to walk through black neighborhoods and promise potential workers high wages and free transportation, medical care, housing, and food. But when the workers arrived in Florida, they were told that they were indebted to United States Sugar for their transportation costs and cane-cutting equipment and could not leave until the debt was paid. The so-called free housing was actually a ramshackle shanty that offered neither privacy nor comfort, and the company routinely cheated them out of pay.[60]

Hurston had witnessed southern peonage firsthand in the turpentine camps, sawmills, lumber companies, and citrus groves of Florida and was thoroughly familiar with the dangers cane cutters faced and the conditions imposed on them by their oppressive employers. Cane cutting was exceptionally dangerous and backbreaking work that began before sunrise and ended after sunset. The machetes that were used were razor sharp, and in spite of the steel-toed boots and aluminum guards cutters were required to wear on their hands, knees, and shins, one in three sustained serious injuries. It was also common to be bitten by fire ants or pierced in the eye or eardrum by a sharp cane leaf.[61]

Eventually, black migration to the northern cities, the war abroad, and the company's indictment for conspiracy to commit slavery made it impossible to recruit African American labor. Rather than reform, in 1943 the company began recruiting laborers from Jamaica, Barbados, and the Bahamas, where jobs were scarce. If a worker refused to comply with United States Sugar policies, the company simply threatened to send him back to abject poverty.[62]

Hurston did some preliminary research on the subject, interviewing a Jamaican supervisor for United States Sugar, but she never wrote the article. As it turned out, nearly ten years later, in 1960, the legendary journalist Edward R. Murrow exposed the brutal exploitation of these migrant workers in one of the most famous documentaries in U.S. history, *Harvest of Shame*. This arresting piece led to better protection for workers.

By the end of February 1951, Zora had completed her final draft of "The Golden Bench of God" as well as a short story about her dog titled "Miss Spot" and had sent them on to Waterbury. Of the novelette, she wrote; "I would pray that it get serialized in one of the big women's mags, but since I have not paid no church dues in quite some time, Old Maker is under no obligation to me whatsoever."[63]

The month of February also brought some progress for Creech's project when Ideal Toy Company president David Rosenstein agreed to mass produce the Saralee doll and help with its marketing. With a manufacturing contract now in place, there was one more hurdle to overcome—the doll's color. Taking Professor Whiting's recommendations for color choice to heart, Creech was left with the impossible task of finding a color for the doll's skin that would reflect the diversity of an entire race. A review of the minutes of the Belle Glade Inter-Racial Council showed that her dilemma was the topic of discussion at the February 4, 1951, meeting, which Hurston attended.

The discussion continued the following Sunday when Howard University president Mordecai Johnson met with Creech and Hurston and other members of the council after a speaking engagement in West Palm Beach. During his visit, Creech, Hurston, and Johnson discussed different solutions for the doll's color, but none seemed to fit. Finally, Creech suggested the creation of a family of dolls that would each be a different shade of brown. In a show of support, Charles S. Johnson offered the assistance of Howard professor Lois Mailou Jones, a renowned Harlem Renaissance artist, who created color sketches of a brother doll and two sisters with differing shades of skin color. Using the sketches as models, Ideal Toy Company made a prototype of each doll.[64]

At Hurston's urging, Creech persuaded Charles Johnson to test the prototypes at Fisk University's faculty day-care center. In the study, sociology department faculty members showed the dolls to a racially mixed group of children and recorded their spontaneous responses.

Although the results were positive, Ideal Toy Company officials felt that producing a family of black dolls was too much of a financial risk and ultimately rejected the idea.[65]

The color problem was eventually solved through the generosity of Eleanor Roosevelt, who offered to host a tea on October 22, 1951, at her Park Avenue Hotel suite for a panel of guests who would serve as a color jury. The members of the jury, who were chosen by Hurston and Creech, included Dr. Charles S. Johnson, Bishop R. R. Wright, Dr. Ralph Bunche, NAACP president Walter White, Dr. Mordecai Johnson, Dr. Benjamin Mays, Lois Mailou Jones, the Urban League's Lester Granger, Sadie Delaney, Mary McLeod Bethune, and Professor Helen Whiting.[66] Sports legend Jackie Robinson was also invited, but neither he nor Zora was able to attend. After a medium-chestnut skin color was chosen, the doll was rushed into production just in time to be included in the 1951 Sears, Roebuck Christmas catalog.

Hurston's hopes for her own cultural breakthrough were still high. When she finally received Waterbury's response to "The Golden Bench," it proved to be disappointing on one hand and encouraging on another. "Miss Spot" did not compel, and the novelette, she advised, would be more marketable as a full-length novel. It was disheartening news to Hurston, whose confidence had been shaken after "Barney Turk" was declined. That failure had left her penniless, and the last thing she wanted to do was again put all of her time and resources into a novel that might never be published. But after thinking it over, she rose to the challenge, telling Waterbury that she had "caught fire" on the idea: "I feel more confident about this story than anything I have done since THEIR EYES WERE WATCHING GOD."[67]

For the next few months, she expanded "The Golden Bench," researched the life of Herod, lectured on folklore at local high schools, and helped Sara Creech paint the outside of her house. "Zora was a fine house painter, and we had fun doing it," Creech recalled. "Mother put on her sun hat, pulled a chair outside and sat beside where we were working to be part of our conversation. It reminded me of a scene right out of *Tom Sawyer*. Before long, a few neighbors brought their chairs and iced tea over and joined in the conversation, too."[68]

The painting project turned out to be a welcome distraction from their various woes. Sara was facing a cancer threat, and Zora was nearly broke. The $600 check from the *American Legion* magazine had gotten lost in the mail, and her rent and car note were coming due. As it turned out, Sara's cancer scare was a false alarm, but the pain and worry over it had soured her otherwise cheerful disposition. Zora tried to rally Creech's spirits, but her well-meaning efforts only back-fired. In a letter to Maxeda von Hesse, Zora admitted to a faux pas that elicited a bitter, but humorous response: "I made the mistake in saying to her [Creech] that no one can be normal mentally when they are physically ill. She did not take to that kindly, pointing out that she has been illish all her born days. It took a few days for her to forgive me for that, though I know that it is true."[69]

Over the next few weeks, Hurston found solutions to her financial woes, but the stress it caused finally took its toll. Waterbury gave her a $100 advance to see her through until the replacement check from the *American Legion* magazine arrived, and Creech loaned her money as well. But at the end of March, her artistic momentum was temporarily halted by a serious bout of the flu. Not hearing from Zora for over a week, Sara drove to the Roof Garden Hotel and found her in a terrible state. Given the serious nature of her condition, Creech took her to the hospital, where she remained for two weeks. She later wrote, "Never have I been so ill since I have been grown."[70] While Zora recovered, Sara took care of Spot. And when the replacement check from the *American Legion* arrived, she paid the balance of Zora's car note as well as her income taxes and rent.

When Zora got back on her feet, she drafted an outline for an article on Senator Robert Taft of Ohio, the leading Republican candidate for the 1952 presidential nomination. She told Waterbury that she had no leanings for or against the candidate before the piece was written but had come to admire him through the course of her research. Besides, the *Saturday Evening Post* seemed to favor Taft, and an article that was favorable to him would be easier to sell them. When the outline was submitted to the magazine for review, however, it became the basis for suspicion of unethical behavior on the part of Waterbury's employer, the Ann Watkins Agency.

According to Zora, someone outside Watkins's office tipped her off that her outline on the Taft article had been given to another Watkins author with the hope that she would be beaten to the draw. The accusation infuriated Zora, who complained to Waterbury: "The first thing too many Negroes do when they want to be writers and public characters in general is to grab something from me, and then hate me for being alive to make their pretensions out a lie. And then take all kinds of steps to head me off. 'Block that Zora Neale Hurston!' is a regular slogan."[71] Hurston's subsequent article, "A Voter Sizes Up Taft," was ultimately sold to the *Saturday Evening Post* and scheduled for publication in its December 8, 1951, issue.

Waterbury claimed that she was finding it increasingly difficult to sell Zora's work. In the 1950s, black writers in general had great difficulty getting their work published, and Zora had the added burden of gender bias and a reputation for being past her prime. In retrospect, her agent also believed that Zora was suffering from a "deterioration of her writing ability" that may have been caused by "her deteriorating state of mind, health, and finances."[72] She claimed that in general, Hurston's articles suffered from "poor organization, lack of focus, and a tendency to degenerate into a diatribe of personal hate."[73]

If that view was shared by others at the Ann Watkins Agency, it might explain why someone may have tried to peddle Hurston's outline to another writer, although there is no evidence to support such a claim. Guilty or not, the scandal took its toll. Jean Parker Waterbury left the Watkins Agency and went solo a few weeks later, and Zora chose to go with her.

By the end of May, Hurston had completed the expanded version of "The Golden Bench of God" and had sent copies to both Mitchell and Waterbury. While she awaited their responses, she began making plans to move to a more permanent home. She had always hoped to return to the little cabin in Eau Gallie where she had written *Mules and Men* (1935), and the timing couldn't have been better. The cabin, located about 100 miles north on the eastern coast, was available for $20 a month, half the rent she was currently paying, and the fees she'd earned from her articles had left her debt free with enough left over to make a new start. Around the end of June 1951, after making arrangements with the cabin's owner, Zora bid the Creeches a fond farewell and she and Spot headed for the beloved home they would share for the next five years.

4

HEROD THE SUN-LIKE SPLENDOR

Eau Gallie, 1951–1956

*Outside of Herod's connection with Christianity, rarely has an
individual appeared who gleamed and glittered from so many
facets. He has impressed himself upon the pages of history as an
athlete, a soldier of the first-class, an equally able administrator,
statesman, a devotee of higher learning, as a great and tragic
lover, and as a friend as famous as Damon and Pythias.*

Hurston's Eau Gallie "farm," as she called it, was not as inspirational
or enduring as Marjorie Kinnan Rawlings's Cross Creek, but it was the
place where she found the privacy, contentment, and peace she had
so longed for. Situated two blocks west of the scenic Indian River and
shaded by palms and moss-draped oaks, her cozy one-room cottage
had a large front porch and an artesian well. The front of the house
faced a paved road, while the back and sides were nestled two blocks
deep in the natural beauty of the Florida landscape.[1]

The cottage, which sat on the corner of Guava Avenue and Fifth
Street (Aurora Road), was located in what had been a black neighborhood when Zora lived there twenty years earlier but was now white.
The property was owned by real estate attorney and Eau Gallie mayor
W. Lansing Gleason, a developer and a member of one of the town's
wealthiest and most pedigreed families. In 1870, Florida lieutenant
governor William Henry Gleason, Lansing's grandfather, had founded
and platted the town, naming it Eau Gallie (Rocky Water) for the co-
quina rock along its shoreline.[2]

By Hurston's measure, the place was in such a dilapidated state
when she arrived that it took "a strong heart" and "an eye on the
future" to muster the courage to move in.[3] No one had lived in the

cottage for quite some time and it had been sorely neglected. The grounds were littered with trash and debris and the exterior was in dire need of paint. Gleason agreed to rent the property to Hurston with the possibility of ownership if she was willing to fix it up. Its condition notwithstanding, in the 1950s it was virtually unheard of for a white property owner to rent to a black tenant in a white neighborhood. To do so could have put both the landlord and tenant at risk of violence or worse. But Gleason's standing in the community and his high regard for Hurston made her an exception, one they hoped the neighbors would support.

Once Zora moved in, she wasted no time in making the place her own. For the first few weeks, with Spot and her pup Shag in tow, she rose before dawn to remove the rubble, clean and paint the house, and begin landscaping. She planted butterfly ginger around the well and replaced the carelessly tossed bottles and cans that littered the yard with pink verbena and colorful poppies. The little money she had in reserve enabled her to purchase a few pieces of furniture, install a birdbath, rewire the house, and transform the empty front porch into a comfortable summer refuge with brightly painted flowerpots, a wooden swing, and some rocking chairs.[4]

Not surprisingly, Zora's cheerful demeanor and pioneering spirit quickly won her neighbors' admiration; they would often stop to compliment her on the improvements she had made. "My neighbors are being very nice to me," she wrote Jean Parker Waterbury. "I think that everything is going to be all right about buying this place."[5] Seeing the time and sweat she was putting into the property, the manager of a local dairy surprised her with a load of compost as a moving-in gift. In less than two months, she'd managed to paint and furnish the house and turn its oak-shaded grounds into a colorful garden with a park-like sweep. She also planted a vegetable garden, installed several bird feeders, and considered putting in papaya trees as a cash crop.

Happier than she had been in a decade, Zora told friends that she was living the kind of life for which she was made, "strenuous and close to the soil."[6] She insisted that gardening, writing, and taking care of her pets had definitely brought her back from the dead. She loved the land and the serenity it provided. Other than the thrum of cicadas and the clamor of birds that gathered in her yard for their daily feeding, there were no loud noises to distract her from her writing. When the peace was broken, it was usually by the thunder of aircraft flying overhead from nearby Patrick Air Force Base: "It is really something to see something that looks like a silver barracuda tearing across the sky ahead of its own sound. As many as I have seen now, the thrill is still strong."[7]

She rarely had visitors, so in early July she was caught off guard by a *Saturday Evening Post* photographer who had been sent to take her picture to accompany the article she had written on Taft. "He caught me in my dungarees working outdoors, and naturally insisted on photographing me like that," she mused.[8]

With the Indian River only blocks away, Zora wore a path to its shores to fish and commune with nature: "The tropical water is so loaded with phosphorus, that standing on the bridge at night, every fish, crab, shrimp, etc., glows as it moves about in the water. When the surface is disturbed, it scintillates like every brilliant jewel you can mention."[9] Considered an ecological treasure, the river's scenic shores remain relatively unspoiled even today. The river, which is actually a long, narrow lagoon fed by saltwater inlets and freshwater creeks, is still home for an abundance of wildlife. Along its shoreline, mangroves provide a rich environment for several varieties of nesting birds and a multitude of marine creatures.

Given the times, if Hurston had not been who she was, her white Eau Gallie neighbors may not have been so tolerant. But Zora was part of that limited firmament of African Americans who were allowed to succeed in the Jim Crow South. Her charm, intelligence, and sense of humor were universal in appeal, and her distinguished career set her apart. And just as Gleason had hoped, her neighbors considered Zora Neale Hurston to be extraordinary. One of those neighbors, Elizabeth Owen, was particularly fond of her. "I had a great admiration for Zora," she declared.[10] Zora and Spot would frequently stop by her house on the way to the post office for a cup of coffee. "She never boasted. Sometimes, when she wasn't able to sell anything, she'd open up her heart and talk."[11] And she was full of surprises. On one of her visits, she wore an authentic Seminole Indian dress and hat. On another, she presented Mrs. Owen with a copy of her novel *Seraph on the Suwanee* with an inscription that read: "To Mrs. Clifford Owen, a throne-angel in a robe of shining rainbows, Zora Neale Hurston."[12] Zora was overly generous with what she had, but she rarely accepted anything in return. "We could never give her anything," Mrs. Owen recalled. "Once, we got a box of typewriter paper for her, but she eventually paid for it."[13]

The Owens knew, as did most of her neighbors, that Zora struggled to make ends meet. In an effort to help, Mr. Owen—who was Eau Gallie's postal express agent—made a gallant attempt to locate Zora's steamer trunk filled with a lifelong collection of anthropological research, manuscripts, and folklore, some of which she hoped to use as a basis for future writing projects. When the trunk had been shipped from New York to Florida several years earlier, Zora had been unable to pay the freight charges. Consequently, it had been labeled "unclaimed" and sent to a warehouse for storage. Owen did everything possible to retrieve it, but too much time had elapsed. By the time he tracked it down, the trunk with its contents had already been sold. It was a great loss, not only to Hurston but to posterity as well.

Always ready to return a kindness, Zora took care of the Owens' home and young daughter Caroline on at least one occasion, during the couple's brief trip to Virginia. And although she was desperate for income, when they tried to pay her she refused, claiming that it had not been work but a pleasure.[14] Owen recalled that Zora had little to give in the way of material things, but she was warm and generous with what she had: "One day, she came in with something in her hand and asked me to hold out mine."[15] When she complied, Zora dropped amaryllis seeds in them. "A tiny gift, but oh, so memorable."[16]

To support herself, in addition to her public appearances, Hurston assembled and trained a cast of local black children and staged a version of her folk concert, "The Great Day." Her "Concert in the Raw," which had originally been performed in 1932 at the John Golden

Theater in New York City, included ballads, work songs, and jook numbers she had collected in the South as well as authentic West Indian folk dancing.

Her first Eau Gallie concert, arranged by Ms. Owen, was staged at a Melbourne High School Parent-Teacher Association meeting. By all accounts, Zora and her performers gave their all-white audience a night to remember; Zora accompanied her cast on the bongo drum. "That was the first time Negroes ever participated on the stage there," Owen enthused.[17]

There were also periods when Hurston would stay indoors for days and refrain from any communication with the outside world. When these episodic "spells of withdrawal" had come over her in childhood, she would sneak into the garden or retreat to her hideout under the house. As an adult, she interpreted these spells as a kind of "creative pregnancy" that preceded a burst of literary ideas. She emerged from one of those spells in August with three short-story ideas adapted from the Bible as well as two articles that she proposed to Waterbury. The first article, "Do Negroes Like Negroes?" was to be a critical look at the black race, while the second article, "Friend Devil, Now," was to be a "tongue-in-cheek exhortation to career women to return to the home lest we lose our ascendancy over men," but there is no evidence that these stories were ever written.[18]

The Owens claimed that they rarely passed Hurston's house without hearing her type, even after midnight. During the fall of 1952, she rewrote two stories on Spot and began the difficult task of trying to shorten her exhaustive Herod manuscript.

Hurston spent at least six years researching the life of King Herod, ruler of Judea from 40 B.C.E. to 4 B.C.E., and about ten years writing about him. Her glorious obsession with his story was an offshoot of her burning desire to write the history of the long struggle of the Jewish people. Throughout history, Hebrews have been referred to as "baby eaters" and "Christ killers," and their consistent refusal to give up their own laws, language, and beliefs and assimilate into the predominant cultures they lived among frequently made them objects of derision and suspicion. They were blamed for the European plague in the 1300s, resulting in hundreds being burned at the stake, and they later suffered genocide under Hitler.

Hurston decried these injustices and the inherent hypocrisy of celebrating Protestant emancipation from the tyranny of the Catholic church during the Reformation while condemning the Jews for revolting against the repressive domination of their corrupt priests in ancient times. Having traced the thread of history through the Bible, the writings of Maccabees and ancient historians, and contemporary Egyptian and Roman histories, she wanted to "show that instead of the Jewish people being a peculiarly evil and hard-headed race of people, doomed by God to suffer and be hated, that they were just people, fighting for all those things which other people hold sacred and conducing to the rights and dignity of man."[19]

In 1945, in a letter to Carl Van Vechten, she wrote: "Beginning with the Sinai, and on to the final destruction of Jerusalem by the Roman emperor Titus (only he was not emperor until later) there was one long and continuous struggle of the people against the arbitrary rule of the priesthood. . . . Moses was responsible for the actual death of at least a half million of the people in his efforts to force his laws upon them."[20]

As an anthropologist, social scientist, and writer who believed in the power of the word, she yearned to give voice to those who had been silenced: "We have no written side of the [Jewish] people other than the direct testimony of their behavior recorded by their oppressors."[21] During their 3,000-year struggle, from the time of their wanderings in the Sinai to the birth of Christ, the Jews were "cut down by the sword of thousands; infested by plague, burnt to death by thousands, decapitated & their heads exposed in the sun; killed by the thousands by poisonous snakes."[22] Referring to the atrocities committed in Europe during the Inquisition, she asserted, "It is a terrible picture and equal to what has gone on in our Christian lands under the Popes and Preachers. A commentary on too much power in any hand, religious or not."[23] She informed Van Vechten that her new work would be titled "Under Fire and Cloud" and solicited his approval: "If you think it should be done, (and I trust your judgement) I am going ahead. I know that it will make thousands mad, but 'Let there be light!'"[24]

How Van Vechten responded is not known, but over the course of her research, Hurston fell in love with Herod's story and decided to make his life and times the focus of her work. After reading the historical works of Titus Livius, Nicolaus of Damascus, and Plutarch, she discovered that this man who she had thought to be "a mean little butcher" was considered to have been a brave soldier; a generous, highly cultivated, and able administrator; and "the handsomest man of his time."[25] Eventually, she came to view Herod as one of the most luminous figures from one of the most lustrous periods in human history.

Beguiled by his genius, she had decided by 1950 to present his story as a play. As she conceived him, Herod's life was not just a story about a "great statesman" and "dashing soldier."[26] Hurston believed that Herod's support for the Essenes, the sect with which Jesus was affiliated, and the protection he provided them from their enemies smoothed the way for the spread of Christianity. "When you review the tenets of the Essenes, that third philosophical sect in Palestine, you will find that everything Christ did or said, according to the Four Gospels was straight from it."[27] As such, his life and historical contributions deserved no less than the big screen. Hoping that her play might be made into a film, she considered actor-director Orson Welles as a possible collaborator and queried Jean Parker Waterbury about any connections she may have had with the famous Hollywood director Cecil B. DeMille. "I know that I sound ambitious, but nothing ventured, nothing gained. I plan to try the LIFE OF HEROD THE GREAT, as a drama, and it needs Hollywood. It is a great story, really, and needs to be done."[28]

Hurston had originally rejected the idea of crafting Herod's story as a biographical novel, fearing that the widely held belief that Herod had ordered infanticide in an effort to kill the infant Jesus would alienate rather than attract readers; his name had long been synonymous with cruelty. But in October 1953, after considering that some of the most popular novels of all time had either been written about or included "detestable characters," she decided to reconsider the idea and solicit Mitchell's support:

> I have been passing through the formative period of my life. Under the spell of a great obsession. The life story of HEROD THE GREAT. You have no idea the great amount of research that I have done on this man, Flavius Josephus, Titus Livius, Eusebius, Strabo, and Nicolaus of Damascus. No matter who talks about him, friend or foe, Herod is a magnificent character. . . . If I can only carve him out as I have conceived him it cannot help but be a good book. . . . So, it is my wish to submit Herod for your inspection, and hope intensely for your approval.[29]

Upon receiving Mitchell's blessing, she began the novel that would ignite her passion and inspire her writing for the remainder of her life.

Convinced of the importance of her subject, she wrote to former British prime minister Winston Churchill to ask him to write the book's introduction as well as a running commentary on the political implications at the end of each chapter. Churchill, citing poor health, graciously declined.

Hurston's enthrallment with the life of Herod was rooted in part in her admiration of the hero and the heroic deed, which she had developed as a child while listening to folktales and reading Greco-Roman myths. Regarding Herod as one of the most vilified and misrepresented heroes in ancient history, she was compelled to set the record straight.

Herod was born in the city of Idumaea in 73 B.C.E. His nearly 40-year reign over Judea is not remembered for its justice but for its indiscriminate cruelty. According to the Gospel of Matthew, his most notorious act was ordering the murder of all male infants in Bethlehem to prevent the fulfillment of a prophecy heralding the birth of the Messiah.[30] Additionally, he ordered the death of a beloved wife and arranged the murders of three of his sons for plotting against him. He was given the appellation "the Great" partly to distinguish him from his descendants with the same name but primarily to honor his indomitable energy and keen political sense.[31] As the linchpin of the Roman Senate's eastern policy, he protected Rome and Judea from its enemies, established a sound bureaucracy, rebuilt roads, opened trade routes, and balanced the demands of Rome against the needs of the Jewish people.[32]

The infamous ruler was also known for the finesse and grandeur of his architectural projects. By the time of his death in 4 B.C.E., the landscape of Judea was dotted with his dazzling cities and fortresses. After an earthquake in 31 B.C.E. nearly destroyed the city of Jerusalem, Herod built the Great Temple and ordered the construction of an amphitheater, a theater, a marketplace, and a building where the Sanhedrin (the Jewish high court) could convene. He also had many buildings constructed in Jericho, Rhodes, Chios, Cos, Samaria, and Lesbos. One of his greatest architectural achievements was the resplendent port of Caesarea, which he named in honor of his friend, Augustus Caesar.[33]

Although it has been widely accepted as truth, there is no historical evidence to support Matthew's claim in the New Testament that Herod (or anyone else) ordered the massacre of male infants.[34] In the absence of evidence, Hurston dismissed the story as inaccurate. Having studied history and religion, she knew that the Synoptic Gospels of Matthew, Mark, and Luke had been written long after the death of Jesus and that even their authorship was uncertain. Legend, she concluded, had stood in for what was not known. Suggesting that Herod had set a bad example that Christians later followed in the bloody crusades, she quipped, "He could not have known that centuries later Christians would themselves slaughter more innocents in one night than his soldiers ever saw."[35]

It seemed ironic to Hurston that Herod was so vilified by Christians when he had paved the way for their religion to flourish. "He trampled upon the Pharisees and the corrupt Sanhedrin mercilessly, [and] highly honored the Essenes, whom all Bible students acknowledge formed the early background of Christianity."[36]

Hurston's proclivity for challenging the status quo had a long (and often contentious) history. Driven by her courage and intelligence, she had lived her entire life pushing the envelope and taking risks in both her personal and literary choices. As Deborah Plant observes, "She was supposed to write about the race problem, but she wrote about the human problem. She was supposed to represent the Intelligentsia, but she spoke for and wrote in the voice of the folk. . . . She lived her passion, not her purse."[37] Therefore, choosing to write about one of the most controversial characters in ancient history and challenging the accuracy of the Bible, a historical record that many believe is the very "word of God," was a gamble she embraced with characteristic verve. As Carla Kaplan reminds us, "When Hurston believed in her material as she did with both 'The Golden Bench of God' and 'Herod the Great,' she was capable of taking tremendous personal risk."[38]

Hurston's search for the true Herod necessarily included the writings of the first-century Jewish historian Flavius Josephus (ca. 37–ca. 100 C.E.), who is considered the primary extant historical source. Other ancient accounts of Herod's life, such as "The Commentaries of Herod the Great," by Herod's "official biographer" Nicholas of Damascus and the writings of the biographer Strabo of Cappadocia, have been lost to the world.[39] Of such importance did Josephus deem the role of Herod that he allotted one-sixth of his total works to him.[40] But after discovering discrepancies between Josephus's account of Herod and those written by Egyptian and Roman historians and in the writings of other biblical scholars such as Titus Livius, Eusebius Plutarch, and Benedict de Spinoza, Hurston adjudged Josephus's work to be a biased source that was poisoned by his religious beliefs.[41] Interestingly, modern biographers such as Peter Richardson and Stewart Perowne have also discovered and challenged those differences.[42]

Hurston's writings suggest that as a traditional Orthodox Jew from a priestly family, Josephus considered Herod, an Arab by birth and a Jew by religious conversion, unworthy of the Judean throne. In her biographical novel she asserts, "It is obvious that the historian, who announces himself as a priest, a Pharisee, and a distant relation of the Asamoneans, looks upon the reign of Herod as something of a sacrilege[,] as did the Bourbons at Napoleon."[43] Since Josephus was born forty years after Herod's death, she was aghast at his presumption that he knew Herod's unspoken motives. She also challenged his characterization of Herod as a Romanized Jew of low birth who usurped the throne of Judea and as a wicked king who "caused the nation to sin" and in so doing created a schism among Jews.[44]

In contrast, in her biographical novel Hurston used more reliable sources to argue that Herod was of royal lineage, having been the son of a princess and an Arab whose family had long enjoyed ducal status.[45] And rather than a Romanized Jew, Hurston asserts—and many modern scholars concur—that Herod was a Hellenized Jew, a progressive Jew who rejected the strict oppressive laws of the ancient Maccabean priests (Orthodox Jews) and assimilated into the Greek culture.[46] Like other Hellenized Jews, Herod attended a Greek university in Damascus, where he studied Greek literature, art, and philosophy. And far from being a usurper of the throne, Hurston protested, his rise to power filled a void left by a civil war begun by the previous ruling family, the Asamoneans, who had fallen out of favor with both the Jewish people and Rome.[47]

Regarding Josephus's prejudicial account of Herod to be a case of "legitimistic spite," Hurston insisted, and accurately so, that when Josephus accused Herod of ushering in the customs of the Gentiles and causing the nation to sin, he blamed the wrong man. In her introduction to "Herod the Great," she reminded readers that Greek culture in Asia existed centuries before Herod's reign. It was given tremendous impetus by Alexander the Great when he crossed the Hellespont with his great army and his scholars in 326 B.C.E.[48] Save for the members of the Jewish priesthood, Hurston wrote, the Hebrew language was lost to the Jews during their captivity in Babylon, resulting in their adoption of the Aramaic language of Persia.[49]

Hurston's reasons for writing about Herod were clearly stated in her preface: "the first being that the West, whose every nation, professes Christianity, should be better acquainted with the real, the historical Herod, instead of the deliberately folklore Herod."[50] Second, she wanted to convey the depths and passion of Herod's love life, which, she claimed, "reaches the height and grandeur of Mount Everest, and touches the depth of Hell."[51]

Hurston considered the political and ideological struggles of the first century B.C.E. to be a political allegory for modern-day Asia, Europe, and America. As evidence, she pointed to the age-old struggle for dominance between the East and West, represented in ancient times by the Parthians, the defenders of the East, and Rome, the champions of the West, "as at present in the world, the mightiest nation of the West, the United States, and the strongest of the East, Soviet Russia, face each other for the minds of men and the mastery of the world."[52] She concluded that the Soviet Union had isolated its country in the same way the Jewish priesthood had created a xenophobic society to maintain cultural purity and authoritative control. "On returning from the Babylonian captivity, they had shut Judea in. The stranger, Gentile[,] was absolutely taboo. . . . The only wa[y] that Ezra and Nehemiah could maintain the absolute priestly rule that they set up, was to keep out knowledge . . . so they set up an iron curtain of their own," she observed.[53]

In Hurston's view, Herod, who was facing an outside threat from Persia and an inside threat from the radical orthodox Jewish priesthood, was in a position similar to that of Chiang Kai-shek in modern-day China. Like Herod, Chiang was facing threats on two fronts: an external threat from the Soviets and an uprising inside China, led by Mao Zedong. Just as Herod had little choice but to turn to Rome for support, Chiang turned to the United States.[54]

Before Herod rose to power, Judea was ruled by a royal family of strict orthodox Jews called the Hasmonean dynasty. Jerusalem was the capital and the king or ruler was the high priest, a position that was passed from father to son.[55] When Herod's birthplace, the Arab-occupied city of Idumaea, was conquered by the Hasmonean king and high priest John Hyrcanus, Herod's family converted to Judaism and began to insert themselves into Jewish politics; Herod's grandfather Antipater was appointed military governor of Idumaea. Upon the death of John Hyrcanus, a struggle over his throne erupted between his sons Aristobulus and Hyrcanus. In an effort to bring stability back into the region and prevent the disruption of trade, Rome captured

Jerusalem, appointed Hyrcanus high priest, and exiled Aristobulus, who died shortly thereafter.[56]

At the time of the Hasmonean uprising, Rome was engaged in its own civil war between Julius Caesar and the Roman general Pompey. Having aligned himself with the victorious Caesar, Herod's father Antipater (who shared his name with Herod's grandfather) was rewarded with the position of governor of Judea, marking the end of theocratic rule.[57]

Hurston began her novel at this definitive time in Herod's life, at age twenty-five, when his father used his position and influence to advance the careers of his two sons. Hurston set the scene: "Standing thus before the congregation, his physical power spoke. In his middle years with a slight brush of grey at his temples, he showed no other sign that he was past his youth."[58] Speaking before the Sanhedrin, Antipater proclaims, "If you will abandon the wicked and destructive practices of this Aristobulus who is now dead and behave toward Hyrcanus as is right and proper, I guarantee that you shall live happily and live your lives without disturbance in the enjoyment of your possessions."[59]

To restore peace and prosperity to Judea, Antipater announced that he had appointed Phasaelus, his first-born son, as governor of Jerusalem, and "to the end that all parts and provinces of our nation be quieted and protected alike, I appoint my second son, Herod, to be governor of Galilee, our most northern province, to put down the tumults there which have come about through the civil strife in the nation and thus gave a handle to those who prefer to live by unlawful means to the injury of honest and pious men."[60] Herod was given the post with the expectation that he would put an end to the murder, rape, and robbery being perpetrated on the cities of Galilee and Syria by a ruthless band of terrorists led by a man named Hezekiah, whom Hurston tells us the people referred to as "the Human Monster."[61]

With his fate and that of Judea resting in the balance, Herod and his troops marched out of the city with great fanfare. Hurston wrote,

"He waved his right hand in salute to the cheering people, flashed his brilliant smile, drew his jewel-hilted sword and waved it above his head as he announced in a loud and convincing voice that the Lion of Judah sought his prey. The people went mad and cheered louder. That was their Herod!"[62]

After he captured and executed Hezekiah, the victorious Herod was considered a hero to some but a villain to others. Many Jews, particularly some of the members of the Sanhedrin, hated Herod and the sectarian laws of his administration. Before Rome reduced the power of the Sanhedrin priests, Jewish religion had dictated the spiritual and legal responsibilities of the Jewish people. Seizing what they hoped would be an opportunity to restore theocratic rule, Hyrcanus and a contingent of Sanhedrin priests conspired with Herod's enemies to bring him to trial for the unlawful murder of Hezekiah.[63]

Hurston told her readers that it was traditional for the criminally accused to appear before the Sanhedrin in black raiment, prostrate themselves, and beg for mercy. In her recreation of the event, Herod defied these customs. On the day of the trial, he entered the chamber wearing his gold-hilted sword and accompanied by 250 loyal soldiers. He wore rich royal purple, gold leather sandals, and glittering gold jewelry. No one dared to rise or speak as he glared into the eyes of each individual. After a lengthy silence, Herod addressed the assembly in an imperious voice: "My generous nature permits you to escape my wrath this time, but if ever again you interrupt my duties as governor of Galilee to ride to Jerusalem to answer your foolish and old-womanish charges, you shall feel the weight of my sword."[64] Thereafter, the matter was put to rest.

After Herod and his men departed, Sameas, a member of the Sanhedrin, proclaimed: "Of this I am persuaded, that one stood before us this day who shall be the master of this nation in no long time."[65] And just as he predicted, Herod's influence and career began to rise. As a strategy to protect Rome's gateway into Asia and to reward Herod for his victory against Hezekiah, Sextus Caesar promoted him to commander of the armed forces of Celesyria.[66] Later, in recognition of his military and administrative genius and, in the words of Octavius

Augustus (Caesar), his "unshakable fidelity to Rome at the repeated risk of his fortune and life," Caesar, Mark Antony, and the Roman Senate proclaimed him king of Judea.[67] When Herod's military campaigns and reign, which extended to all of western Asia, had provided Judea with "security and peace and such wealth as the nation ha[d] never seen before in all its history," Caesar awarded him with the designation "Herod Magnus[;] Herod the Great."[68]

Hurston's admiration and passion for her subject is clearly discernable throughout her novel, particularly in passages that describe the erotic feelings Herod evoked in women. For instance, Hurston imagined the reaction of the adolescent Mariamne, who was destined to be Herod's second wife and greatest love, when she saw the "handsome, strong, and masterful" Herod as he rode up a hill toward the palace: "Her body grew hot all over as she watched the horseman gallop by. Her developing breasts that became tight and thrust forward required the touch of Herod's long, strong hands to smooth. If only by some miracle his hands could find their way to her throbbing breasts, the strange pains would go away."[69] Relying on historical accounts, Hurston described another occasion when Herod's alluring physique cast a spell on the "beautiful, witty, and charming" Egyptian queen Cleopatra, who sent him a small strip of papyrus on which was written, "To the man with the most beautiful eyes and lips upon the earth. And to the arms most fitted for love."[70]

Hurston the folklorist is also present in this novel. In a scene reminiscent of a jook joint rendition of "Uncle Bud," Herod's soldiers break out with a ballad titled "Joseph, the Camel Rider."[71]

Of the ten wives Herod took over the course of his life, his second wife Mariamne was the most beloved and ultimately the most tragic. In Hurston's novel, Herod describes his love in lofty and tender terms: "A love superior to any felt by any man since the beginning of the world now possesses me for Mariamne. . . . It is not only her beauty, but a female softness, warmth, her helplessness and dependence upon my strength. . . . She is more than a mere wife to me. She is my woman."[72] But his love was doomed. Prompted by her mother Alexandra, Mariamne devised a plot to have Herod murdered. When she was caught and found guilty of treason, Herod ordered her death, a decision that almost drove him to madness.[73]

Despite Hurston's efforts to lighten the work in words and tone, the unwieldy nature of the material weighed it down. In utter frustration she complained to Mitchell, "You have no idea how I have struggled to shorten this work, and with a literary hop and jump place Herod on the throne and march on to the end of the work with no more than 80,000 words. But it just will not come out that way."[74]

While she continued to labor on "Herod," she received word from Mitchell that "The Golden Bench of God" had been declined. While her protagonist, Madame Walker, was "a warm, attractive character," Mitchell explained, the editors felt that "the book as a whole" would not be successful.[75] Instead of a revision, Mitchell urged her once again to write another volume of her autobiography. After Scribner's rejection, Jean Parker Waterbury submitted the story to Tay Hohoff, an editor at J. B. Lippincott, but Hohoff came to the same conclusion: the work just wasn't up to par.

Since no copies of the "The Golden Bench" survive, it is impossible to ascertain whether Hurston's writing ability had in fact declined or whether her publishers were passing on the novel for other reasons. Was her subject matter problematic for a white readership? Did the 1948 scandal make publishing her work risky? Did the stress of her financial woes and her declining health adversely affect her writing ability? In an interview with Robert Hemenway, Waterbury recalled, "She could write like an angel and yet be absolutely sloppy when she was desperate for money. . . . She would lose all sense of perspective and judgment, and just as long as there were words on the page she felt that she could get some cash for it."[76]

While the answers to these questions remain speculative, one fact remains: Hurston consistently refused to allow failure to diminish her spirit. She took the rejection well and assured Waterbury and Hohoff that they need not handle her with "kid gloves." No doubt influenced by the disappointment, Zora scrapped her short-story ideas and, as Mitchell had suggested, began "bunching her muscles" to tackle the second volume of her autobiography. In defiance of what must have been an enormous letdown, she remained in good spirits and looked forward to a visit by her nephew, Everett. "Let's plan one whale of a Thanksgiving Day. Big games, dinner, dancing, etc," she urged.[77]

Everette's visit never occurred, and the remaining months of 1951 were fraught with financial difficulties. In October, she had hoped to attend a tea hosted by Eleanor Roosevelt in New York City to help select a color for the Saralee doll, but with no money coming in, she had neither the means nor the leisure to go. Sara Creech would have gladly paid her way, but Zora was too proud to allow it. Faced with an empty pantry and a paltry income, she hocked her typewriter and borrowed another to keep on writing. Her plans to buy her Eau Gallie haven were also thwarted. Even if she could have obtained the needed funds, a dispute among the late owner's heirs had resulted in a lawsuit that threatened to tie up the title of the property for years.

The new year began on a more optimistic note when Lippincott sent her a small royalty payment of $37.87 for the reprinting of *Their Eyes Were Watching God* in Scandinavia. The translation rights brought in a stipend as well. She earned some additional income during the first few weeks of 1952 by staging five folk concerts throughout the community, but the effort proved greater than the financial return. Had she been inclined to continue the concerts, a sudden bout of illness in February that left her weak as a kitten would have stopped her in her tracks. She had suffered these periodic episodes since her return from Honduras. Her doctors attributed the symptoms, which included headache, fatigue, and swelling of the underarms and groin, to a tropical virus that they believed she had contracted from drinking the water there. Given the nature of the illness, there was nothing they could do but assure her that the virus was cyclical and hope that this latest bout would be her last.

By the first week in March, she was feeling better and considering an offer to participate in a debate that was to take place in Boston between Robert Taft and Dwight Eisenhower. She was willing to go, but a lack of warm clothes, particularly a coat, made the trip impractical. She declined an invitation to work on the Citizens for Taft Committee in New York for similar reasons. In lieu of travel, she put a great deal of thought and research into her ideas for two articles. One was on the cattle business in Florida and the other was a rather ambitious political and social analysis of the underlying causes of the "anti-Anglo-Saxon feeling in Asia and the Near East."[78] As it turned out, neither was published.

Over the months that followed, barely able to make ends meet, she grew most of her food, attended city commission meetings, corresponded with Herbert Sheen and other friends and family, and continued to write. In May, she told Mitchell that she was working on the second volume of her autobiography (which was never completed) and had accepted an offer to write a column for *The Weekly Review*, a Negro newspaper in Augusta, Georgia. The opportunity to earn a regular income, life on her farm, and a new sense of purpose had raised her spirits considerably. In her letter to Mitchell, she proclaimed, "Getting out in the yard and growing things has been a marvelous release for me so that now I feel fine inwardly and receiving letters from the upper brackets of Negroes from all over the country letting me see that I stand high with them has been helpful too. So now you can consider me definitely back from the dead."[79]

In late September 1952, things took an unexpected turn when Zora received a job offer that led to what many judge to be her best literary writing of the period. This momentous assignment took her deep into the bowels of Ku Klux Klan territory to Live Oak, Florida, to cover the murder trial of a black woman named Ruby McCollum, who had walked into the medical office of her white lover, Dr. Leroy Adams, and shot him dead. The murder had garnered national headlines as one of the most sensational trials in the history of the South, and the *Pittsburgh Courier* offered Zora $1,000 to cover the court proceedings and write a ten-part biographical sketch of Ruby's life. It was a dangerous assignment, particularly for a black female reporter; Live Oak was crawling with Klansmen who hated any meddling by journalists and made threats against anyone, black or white, who talked to them. Never being one to shrink from a challenge, Hurston accepted the assignment, packed her bags, and headed straight for the center of a hornet's nest.

Above: Hurston with her new Chevrolet—furnished by her patron Charlotte Osgood Mason—on a folklore expedition in the South in 1928. (Courtesy of Dorothy West Collections, Boston University)

Left: Sara Creech with her Saralee doll, 2003. (Courtesy of Sara Lee Creech)

First lady Eleanor Roosevelt and guests examine models of the Saralee doll at her Park-Sheraton Hotel suite in New York City on October 26, 1951. Mrs. Roosevelt hosted a tea for her guests, who served as a jury to select the doll's proper color. Seated from left are Sara Creech, the doll's creator; Maxeda von Hesse; Walter White, executive director of the National Association for the Advancement of Colored People; Mrs. Roosevelt; and Dr. Ralph Bunche, winner of the Nobel Prize for Peace and director of the United Nations Department of Trusteeship. (Courtesy of Sara Lee Creech)

Mary Creech, with whom Zora spent hours in the Creech family library researching the life of King Herod. (Courtesy of Sara Lee Creech)

First page of a January 1942 article in *Ebony* magazine, "Modern Designs for Negro Dolls: Manufacturers Find Trends More Realistic." Bottom left: Patti-Jo. Top from left: Saralee doll, Amosandra, Jackie Robinson, Harlem dancing doll. Bottom Right: Auntie Belinda and a rag doll. (Courtesy of Sara Lee Creech and *Ebony* magazine)

An Indian River fishing hole located two blocks east of the location of Hurston's Eau Gallie cottage. (Photo by the author)

Isaiah Hurston's home in Sanford, where Zora completed her first novel, *Jonah's Gourd Vine*, in 1934. (Photo by the author)

The residence of Zora's father, John Cornelius Hurston, in Sanford on the corner of Hickory and 6th Street, which he owned as early as 1908. (Photo by the author)

Above: A view from the balcony of the Suwannee County Courtroom, where the trial of Ruby McCollum was held in 1952. (Photo by the author)

Left: William Bradford Huie, early 1950s. Courtesy of Martha Hunt Huie.

A view from the banks of the Indian River just west of the site where Hurston's Eau Gallie cottage was located. (Photo by the author)

Zora and her typewriter in her Eau Gallie cottage. (Courtesy of *The Saturday Evening Post*)

Lee Sarah Peek Funeral Home in Fort Pierce, location of Hurston's funeral in 1960. (Courtesy of Suzanne Antonetti, photographer)

Former *Fort Pierce Chronicle* building in Fort Pierce, where Hurston was employed as a reporter in 1956. (Courtesy of Suzanne Antonetti, photographer)

Hurston's final home at 1734 School Court in Fort Pierce. (Courtesy of Suzanne Antonetti, photographer)

Former home of Beanie Backus, where Hurston was frequently a guest along with other artists and musicians. (Courtesy of Suzanne Antonetti, photographer)

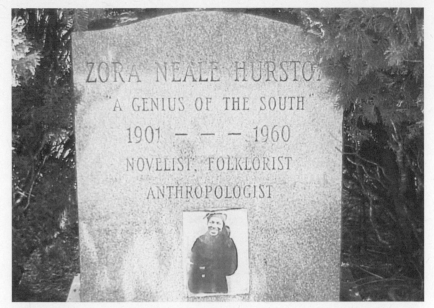

Hurston's tombstone and grave site at what is currently Sarah's Memorial Garden Cemetery in Fort Pierce. (Photo by the author)

Hurston's coffin with pallbearers (*Fort Pierce Chronicle*, 1960)

Flower girls, Hurston's funeral (*Fort Pierce Chronicle*, 1960)

Hurston's gravesite processional with Sara Creech in the forefront (*Fort Pierce Chronicle*, 1960)

Hurston's funeral procession with pallbearers (*Fort Pierce Chronicle*, 1960)

5

DEATH ON THE SUWANNEE

Live Oak, 1952–1953

*The dumbest thing a woman can do is to refuse to fade out
of the picture when the man is through with her. . . .
She was a woman terribly in love, and with us females,
that makes strange and terrible creatures of us.*

The facts surrounding the McCollum trial had all the elements of a
best-selling novel: forbidden love, deep betrayal, insatiable greed, political corruption, bizarre revelations, and bloody murder. Hurston accepted the *Pittsburgh Courier*'s offer out of a need for cash, but she was
also drawn by a genuine fascination with the "dramatics of the case
and the varied play of human emotions."[1]

The defendant, Ruby McCollum, was a 37-year-old mother of four
who was married to "Bolita Sam" McCollum, the wealthiest black man
in town. Sam and Ruby had made a fortune running a wildly popular
and profitable (albeit illegal) numbers game called bolita (Spanish for
"little ball"), a forerunner of today's lotto. The game had been popular
since 1942, when it had found its way to the United States from Cuba.
By 1950, it had become a statewide obsession and a powerful source
of wealth for those associated with its operation.

The murder victim, 44-year-old Dr. Clifford Leroy Adams, was a
husband and father, a shrewd politician, a state legislator-elect, and
by all accounts the most popular physician in Suwannee County. The
tall pot-bellied physician, whom Hurston described as "a broad-shoul-
dered six-footer with magnificence of body," had been Ruby's lover for
six years and had fathered her one-year-old daughter Loretta.[2] Ruby

also claimed to be pregnant with their second child at the time of the murder. Ultimately, due largely to Hurston's insight and perseverance, Dr. Adams was exposed as an incompetent physician who was himself capable of murder as well as profound cruelty and greed.

Ruby McCollum shot Dr. Adams on August 3, 1952, a quiet Sunday morning. After making his hospital rounds, Adams went to his office across the street from the Suwannee County Courthouse to see a few waiting patients. Shortly afterward, Ruby pulled her blue two-tone Chevy into the alley near the colored entrance behind his office. With her two young children, Loretta and Sonya, in the back seat, nineteen $100 bills in her purse, and a nickel-plated .32 caliber Smith and Wesson pistol in her brown shoulder bag, she paced outside his office, waiting to catch the doctor alone. After a few hours, unwilling to wait any longer, Ruby entered his office and burst into an examination room to confront him.[3]

According to witnesses, Ruby gave Dr. Adams a $100 bill, demanded a receipt, and bitterly complained that she was tired of paying him money that she didn't owe. In response, Adams insisted that she owed him more than $100 and said that he was damn well going to get what was coming to him. With his last words still hanging in the air, Adams turned away from Ruby and walked toward the waiting room, where three women were waiting to be seen. As soon as the doctor's back was turned, Ruby assured him that he was in fact going to get what was coming to him. With the wrath of a woman scorned, she removed the gun from her purse and shot Adams three times as he fell to the floor and once more when he hit it.[4]

When the shots were fired, the three horrified women in the waiting room bolted into the alley screaming for help. With the gun still smoking in her hand and the $100 bill still clutched in his, Ruby stepped over her former lover, got into her car, and drove home. With zombie-like motions she changed her dress, fed her baby, and calmly waited for the sheriff and his deputies to arrive.[5]

White resident Laura Helventon, who was in her early teens at the time, was with her family in the Methodist church next door to Dr. Adams's office when the murder took place. "After the shots rang out, everyone was shocked and scared. The Reverend Philpot refused to allow anyone to leave the church until the source of the gunfire was determined," she recalled.[6] When Dr. Adams's murder was announced, the horrified congregation let out a collective gasp of disbelief. Later that day, nearly a hundred Klansmen came out of hiding to walk the streets. Their ominous presence cast a pall over the entire community and served as a warning to black residents to stay out of sight. In an effort to quell the mounting tension, a large contingent of state highway patrolmen was dispatched to keep an all-night vigil as a safeguard against further violence.

When news of the murder reached Ruby's husband, he gathered up his three young daughters, took a reported $85,000 from his safe, and fled to Ruby's mother's home near Ocala.[7] But physical escape could not allay his mental anguish. The next day, 47-year-old Sam suffered a massive heart attack and died, taking the whereabouts of the money he took from his safe to his grave.[8]

When Hurston arrived in Live Oak in late September, she found a deeply segregated, traumatized community. Lynchings still took place in Florida. And at the time of Adams's murder, Floridians were still reeling from several violent incidents that had raised racial tensions to an all-time high. In 1949, two black men had been shot and killed in Groveland after being accused of abducting and raping a 17-year-old married white woman named Norma Padgett. Her accusation against four black men had set off four days of rioting by angry white mobs, which sent terrified black residents fleeing for their lives. Dubbed "Florida's little Scottsboro," the case became a cause célèbre after Sheriff Willis V. McCall, the most feared lawman in the country, shot two of the handcuffed defendants while transporting them to a hearing.[9] Two years later, on Christmas Eve in 1951, Harry Tyson Moore, NAACP secretary for the state of Florida and the one who had led the successful drive to register black voters in the state, and his wife were killed when the Ku Klux Klan detonated a bomb under their Sanford, Florida, home. It was the Moores' twenty-fifth anniversary. Harry died almost immediately, but his wife lingered for nine days. Moore was the first NAACP activist to be killed in the civil rights movement.

As Hurston would discover, the potential for violence in Suwannee County was increased by the fear that the facts surrounding Adams's murder would come to light. In addition to his illicit affair with Ruby (miscegenation was then a crime), it was widely believed that Dr. Adams was a member of a white syndicate of bolita front men who shared in the game's profits. As Sam's business manager and bookkeeper, Ruby had meticulously recorded the names and payoff amounts to those who fronted the operation in a secret ledger, as well as the names of the local and state officials paid to look the other way.[10]

Ruby told her attorneys that Adams had been extorting bolita profits. After Adams was murdered, a cover-up began to protect those who were involved in the racket, including law enforcement officials, state and local politicians, and businessmen. The Klan enforced a strict code of silence, and the trial judge and state prosecutor joined forces with local law enforcement officials to whitewash the facts and derail the press. Because reporters were seen as threats, the judge relentlessly and shamefully violated Ruby's First Amendment rights by refusing to allow her access to the press.

The circumstances surrounding the case made Hurston's assignment not only difficult but downright dangerous. Digging for facts would have put any reporter at risk, much less one who was black and female. Most of the local black folks were furious with Ruby for stirring up the Klan. And many residents, including white folks, felt that Ruby had deprived them of Dr. Adams's promise to keep them in high cotton in return for their political support. But in spite of the dangers, the ever-fearless Hurston was determined to uncover the facts.

Zora's weekly coverage of the trial began on October 11, 1952, with Ruby McCollum's sanity hearing and continued through January 17, after the trial had ended. Her dramatic and at times humorous descriptions of the proceedings first appeared in the *Pittsburgh Courier* on October 11 under the title "Zora's Revealing Story of Ruby's 1st Day in Court." From her seat in the balcony (the colored section), Hurston had a bird's-eye view of the courtroom and an earful of atmosphere. She described the courthouse as "clean and comfortable," with separate buckets of ice water and dippers for blacks and whites (though the buckets for blacks were seldom filled). Spittoons were also provided for tobacco and snuff users.

At the sanity hearing Zora observed that while the local black community largely shunned the proceedings, the balcony was lined with out-of-town spectators from as far south as Fort Lauderdale, almost 378 miles away. The downstairs area, where the white folks sat, was equally packed, including the chairs to the right of the bench where visiting lawyers and a former governor were seated. Some even brought their knitting, which Zora likened to the ladies of the French Revolution "who brought their knitting and worked away as they cheered" while the "bloody heads fell into the basket."[11]

Known for her clever use of courtroom drama for symbolic effect in works such as "Mule Bone," *Their Eyes Were Watching God*, and "Conscience of the Court," she employed the technique when reporting the banter (which she lifted wholesale from the porch dwellers in *Their Eyes*) of a reproachful balcony spectator to set the tone: "'Colored women ought to be proud to stick to their own men and leave these white men alone. And more specially when they ought to know that white men ain't no trouble at all. They can't do nothing in bed but praise the Lord. Nothing to 'em at all.'"[12]

Out of the cast of characters, Hurston considered the trial judge, Hal W. Adams, to be the most colorful, describing him as "a man possessed of many substances marketable in the human bazaar."[13] Considered an exemplar of a southern institution, Judge Adams was an emaciated 70-year-old Florida cracker with long shaggy eyebrows and shoulder-length hair. He wore a black Stetson hat, a dark suit with a long coat, an old-fashioned string tie, and high-topped shoes. Throughout the proceedings, he kept a chaw of tobacco in his jaw while dispensing jokes and homilies as he proudly demonstrated his skill in hitting his chairside spittoon. He was a courtly gentleman with an extravagantly courteous southern manner and a propensity for calling all white men "brother."[14] Although he was not related to Dr. Adams, he had been the doctor's political ally, friend, and pallbearer. Given their close association, he should have recused himself from the case at the outset.

Zora's coverage of the trial was lively, vivid, and colorful. She described prosecutor Keith Black—who often wore rumpled suits—as a short, plump man with a bald spot on the crown of his head "so round and exact that it might have been the tonsure of a monk."[15] When he was seated, he was quiet. "But when he moved or spoke, he emitted alertness so intense it was electrical," she observed.[16] At least one of the local spectators agreed, telling Zora: "That man is a getting fool. Never mind about that bald head and him being short and squaddly. He can go for broke. I done heard him at it."[17] Zora described Ruby's first attorney, P. Guy (Pig Eye) Crews, as a heavyset gentleman with a "hounddog" expression and eyes that sloped down so sharply in the corners "one got the impression that a slight blow, and his eyeballs would run down into his collar."[18]

In her second *Courier* article, "Ruby Sane!" published October 18, 1952, Zora's impression of Ruby was that of a proud, rather plain-looking, self-contained woman. "Well-dressed and groomed, she is the kind who would best be described as attractive." Toward the end of her article, referring to gossip that Ruby was the jealous type, Hurston pondered, "Could that be the explanation, in part, for what took place in the office of Dr. Adams on August 3?" The truth would prove infinitely more complicated.

Over the course of the trial, which ended on December 20, 1952, Hurston gathered information for her biographical series on the life of Ruby and sprinkled it throughout her courtroom coverage for dramatic effect. The strictly imposed code of silence had little effect on Zora's talent for getting people to talk, even under the most extreme circumstances. Most of the biographical material came from Ruby's attorneys, friends, and family members, who revealed her to be a well-educated, intelligent, ambitious, and calculating woman who was attracted to powerful men.

Hurston's biographical series on Ruby McCollum, which ran weekly from February 28 to May 2, 1953, was not only seasoned with Hurston's characteristic rich descriptions and folksy phrases, like her trial coverage, it was also embellished with lines from her previous novels. In her fourth installment, Hurston used the same lines she had written about her characters Tea Cake and Janie to describe the relationship between Sam and Ruby: "Sam made a little summertime out of seemingly nothing and they both lived off it for hours that they were together. . . . Silently unsatisfied by her narrow surroundings, she had been fumbling around with the door-knob of life and Sam McCollum had opened the door."[19] As brassy as it was, these borrowed phrases made the existing drama all the more titillating.

One of the more amusing stories Hurston penned in her series "The Life Story of Mrs. Ruby J. McCollum" was about the McCollums's establishment in Live Oak in 1936. "The coming of the McCollums to Live Oak was so quiet and inconspicuous that even Negro Live Oak was scarcely conscious that they were there," she wrote.[20] One day while driving around their new town, Ruby noticed a big two-story yellow stucco home on Ninth Street. The house belonged to a fellow named Hopps, a local bolita banker who was one of the wealthiest black men in town. She told Sam that she had seen that house in a dream and that someday it would be hers. Later on, seizing an opportunity to secure their future, Sam won the house in a poker game. "People in Live Oak still tell of that night when Sam and Hopps sat down at the gambling table and fought with their skills for what was left. When the air cleared, Sam was the master of the big house on Ninth Street, and Hopps—clean as a fish—walked out of town with his coat over his arm."[21]

In addition to his bolita kingdom, Sam McCollum amassed one of the largest tobacco acreage allotments in Florida, acquired several rental properties, and served as the director of the highly profitable Central Life Insurance Company. It was rumored that Sam and Ruby had so much money coming in that on any given day there was as much as $100,000 stashed away in the family's two vaults. Ruby's nephew Carlton Jackson said that when he visited his aunt as a child, he was bewildered by the "stacks of money" all over the place. "I used to wonder where it all came from, and why it was there."[22]

Hurston abhorred Ruby's act of murder, yet in the fifth installment of her biographical series, she seemed to sympathize with Ruby's plight as a neglected wife. She intuited that for all her wealth,

Ruby was lonely and vulnerable when she met Dr. Adams in 1945.[23] It was no secret that Sam had neglected Ruby for younger women. Their marriage had unofficially ended when their only son, Sam, Jr., was seven years old and Ruby was five months pregnant with their oldest daughter, Kay. According to Hurston's sources, things came to a head one evening around Christmas when, over Ruby's objections, Sam invited some so-called business associates over to the house for some drinks and card playing. As the night rolled on, the raucous crowd got ruder and drunker until finally several inebriated guests vomited on the floor. A horrified Ruby took her husband aside to protest in private. But instead of putting an end to the evening as she had expected, a clearly irritated Sam demanded that she stop bellyaching and clean it up. When Ruby refused, Sam beat his pregnant wife into submission.[24]

Using yet another line from *Their Eyes*, Hurston described Ruby's feelings after the beating in the same way she described Janie Crawford's after her husband Jody Starks struck her: "An image—something sacred and precious—had fallen off the shelf in Ruby's heart."[25] Thereafter, Ruby and Sam continued to live together but in separate bedrooms.

Hurston believed that Dr. Adams was attracted to Ruby's money and that she was flattered by his attention. They kept their affair secret until Ruby's third daughter Loretta was born, the spitting image of Dr. Adams. This came as a great shock to Sam, whose pride was deeply hurt. As Hurston noted, it was okay for him to run around town flaunting his "young gals" on his arm, but he expected his wife to uphold a different standard.[26] They continued to work together as parents and business partners, but Sam made it clear that he would kill her if she continued the affair.

Over time, as Dr. Adams's political ambitions grew, he became physically and mentally abusive toward Ruby, seeing less and less of her and more and more of his 20-year-old white girlfriend, Evelyn Anderson. When Ruby saw what was happening, it cut her deeply. She became a neurotic hypochondriac who was physically and emotionally dependent on Dr. Adams, often calling him as many as seventeen times a day. Her mental instability was so severe that on three occasions Dr. Adams had her admitted to Brewster Hospital in Jacksonville for treatment.

Ruby was wealthier and better educated than most of the blacks in her community, which made her an object of considerable envy. Hurston, who hated black-hearted gossip more than barbwire pie, decried black residents who publicly criticized Ruby for having a white lover. She considered their gossip a cowardly tactic staged to appease members of the white community who might overhear them: "These local Colored people were, for the most part, little people, the kind of people irrespective of race, who have only the earth as their memorial. The sprig of hyssop was in their hands, and they were sprinkling the blood of the paschal lamb around their doorways so that the Angel of Death would pass over them. This, never you forget, was West Florida."[27]

Hurston's disdain was deepened by her own experiences. Her correspondence with friends is rife with expressions of bitterness toward her race for what she viewed as a propensity for cruelty and hatred toward any Negro who achieved success: "Not my supposed *White enemies*, but *Negroes*, have played every vile trick upon me that can be imagined, without rhyme or reason except hating to see me reap any benefit from hard work."[28]

Ruby's trial began December 16 after P. Guy Crews was disbarred for unrelated unethical behavior and replaced with a new attorney, Frank Cannon, a former county prosecutor from Jacksonville. Unlike Crews, Cannon was well dressed, tall, graceful, and handsome. When the proceedings ultimately got under way, Hurston described the two as they appeared together in the courtroom: "Black looked like a well-fed mule beside a race horse with Cannon."[29] But the spectators didn't come alive until Ruby McCollum was escorted into the packed courtroom, tastefully dressed and expressionless.

At five foot three, Ruby was a small woman who held herself with dignity and self-control. Throughout the trial, Hurston reported only one instance when Ruby exhibited any emotion. It was during her testimony about the actual slaying: "Ruby did not break down and weep; she did not scream out in an agony of memory; but there was an abrupt halt in her testimony as emotion gushed up from the deeps of her soul and inhabited her face. I saw it: the quintessence of human agony."[30] Ruby had already confessed to the murder, so the purpose of the trial was to determine the degree of guilt by hearing her own testimony concerning her motives. And since the judge refused to instruct the jury to consider a second-degree murder verdict, it was all or nothing.

When Ruby took the stand, other than her account of the murder, all that she was allowed to say was that she and Dr. Adams had been lovers and that her daughter Loretta was his. The state attorney and the judge joined forces to ensure that the jury heard nothing else that could hurt the doctor's reputation or mitigate the circumstances of his murder. Contrary to the account of the eyewitnesses, Ruby testified that she had gone to Dr. Adams's office on the morning of the murder to request treatment for shoulder pain. She claimed that after giving her a shot, the doctor had told her that she owed him $16 for the shot plus a balance of $100. She had disputed the balance, but had given in to his demands and handed him a $100 bill. After writing a receipt, Ruby insisted that Dr. Adams had produced a gun, held it to her belly, and demanded that she have sex with him on an examination table. When she refused, he had hit her twice, and she had shot him out of fear.

Defense attorney Frank Cannon asked Ruby thirty-eight questions pertaining to her statements about the doctor's physical and mental abuse and about his attempts to extort bolita money from her. And thirty-eight times state attorney Keith Black objected and thirty-eight times Judge Hal W. Adams sustained the objection. In her commentary on the trial, a clearly disgruntled Hurston declared: "My comprehensive impression of the trial was one of a smothering blanket of silence. . . . It was as if one listened to a debate in which everything which might lead to and justify the resolution had been waived. . . . It amounted to mass delusion by unanimous agreement."[31]

Hurston sympathized with Cannon's growing frustration and anger and was herself stupefied as she listened and watched Judge

Adams and state attorney Black suppress testimony that could have saved Ruby's life. Zora wrote that at one point, a visibly angry Frank Cannon told the judge: "May God forgive you, Judge Adams, for robbing a human being of life in such a fashion. I would not want it on my conscience."[32]

The state contended that Ruby had killed Adams over a contested doctor's bill. The defense argued that Ruby had shot Adams out of self-defense. On the morning of the murder, Ruby had an envelope clutched in her hand. Although the defense said it was a billing statement, the doctor's office clerk testified that she had not mailed a bill to the McCollums' home. The envelope, addressed to Sam in Dr. Adams's own handwriting, had arrived in the McCollums' post office box the Saturday morning before the murder. Hurston and others speculated that it was a demand by Adams for a higher share of bolita profits. Not surprisingly, Ruby's brown purse with the envelope and the eighteen remaining $100 bills in it mysteriously disappeared sometime between Ruby's arrest and her booking into Raiford State Prison.

At the trial's conclusion, the all-white jury, which included six of the doctor's former patients, came back with a guilty verdict with no recommendation for mercy. Ruby McCollum was sentenced to death by the electric chair on January 23, 1953. Ending her commentary on a bitter, sarcastic note, Hurston wrote: "The trial was ended. A Negro woman had become infuriated over a doctor bill, and she had killed the good doctor . . . the friend of the poor . . . a man whose only rule had been the Golden Rule. And now the poor men would have their justice: Their eye for an eye and tooth for a tooth. The Community will had been done."[33]

Zora's vexation was intensified when the *Pittsburgh Courier* left her high and dry by failing to pay her any of the money they had promised other than the initial $200. As a result, she had to wait two days after the trial ended for the *Courier* to send her the money needed to return to Eau Gallie. To make matters worse, the tension and stress of the case caused her sinus and gall-bladder trouble to come down on her with terrible force, and she had no money for medical care.

Her coverage of the McCollum trial had also cost her an invitation to participate in the annual Florida Folk Festival held in nearby White Springs.

But although the trial had ended, the McCollum case and her involvement in it was far from over. When the verdict was read, Frank Cannon wasted not a minute before filing an appeal with the Florida Supreme Court on fifty-eight points of trial irregularities. Hurston knew that Cannon was going to need all the help he could get. Despite the fact that he had been born in Suwannee County, Cannon was branded a public enemy, and the locals were already measuring him for the undertaker. Unwilling to accept the verdict of a kangaroo court but unable to do any more, she called upon journalist William Bradford Huie to come to the rescue.

Huie and Hurston, who were both native Alabamans, had become friends when he was the associate editor and later editor of the *American Mercury* magazine, a New York publication co-founded by H. L. Mencken, for which Hurston had written several articles in the mid-1940s. Throughout his career, Huie, one of the few white southern writers who joined the 1960 crusade for civil rights, claimed to be in the "truth business." At the time of the McCollum trial, he had written a successful autobiographical novel, *Mud on the Stars* (1942), and was in the process of publishing *The Execution of Private Slovik* (1954), a controversial book about the first American soldier executed for desertion since the Civil War. He had also published articles condemning the castration of Edward Aaron and the lynching of fourteen-year-old Emmett Till and had made many enemies in Alabama when he wrote his 1967 novel *The Klansman*. His most controversial book was written in 1970 about the investigation of the Martin Luther King assassination. Huie wrote twenty novels in his lifetime, in addition to a book on the McCollum case: *Ruby McCollum: Woman in the Suwannee County Jail* (1956), to which Hurston contributed. Although most of his books are out of print, over 28 million copies were sold, and eight of his books were made into films.

In January 1954, at Zora's request, Huie agreed to stop in Live Oak to "pry casually into the story" on his way to Fort Myers, Florida, where he and his wife Ruth had planned to vacation. But those plans changed when Judge Adams refused to allow him to talk to Ruby, who had been in jail for eighteen months while her case was on appeal. "I was threatened, investigated, cussed as a 'traitor' and an 'outsider.' I was denounced as a 'meddler' and an 'interloper.' I was called a Communist and a 'nigger lover.' My wife was accused of being 'part nigger.' I was compelled to fight."[34]

With the battle lines drawn, Huie was committed to giving the judge the utmost outside interference he could muster. What ensued was a long eye-gouging battle over Ruby's civil rights. Huie threatened to go to the U.S. Supreme Court over the judge's gag ruling, and Judge Adams threw Huie in jail for contempt of court. But just as Hurston had hoped, Huie was hell-bent on ferreting out the truth in the McCollum case; he began by interviewing any and everyone who was willing to reveal it.

Hurston continued to encourage, aid, and correspond with Huie during his long investigation, in defiance of purported threats against her by the Ku Klux Klan.[35] In addition to her notes, advice, and leads on the McCollum case, she also shared with Huie her passion for her Herod story and hopes for its successful publication. As a token of friendship, he sent her an inscribed copy of his novel *The Execution of Private Slovik*.

As Huie's investigation continued, he discovered that Dr. Adams was a member in good standing of the Ku Klux Klan. He had also been an incompetent physician, according to Dr. Russell Count, a physician who had worked with him. Count told Huie that he had seen Adams amputate a leg using unsanitary techniques and remove an appendix without first determining whether the patient's white cell count was elevated enough to indicate infection.[36] According to Dr. Adams's nurse, Edith Parks, he never prepared or read anything before surgery, although he did have some skill in obstetrics and gynecology. She also claimed that he had no respect for the poor folks to whom he promised jobs. He'd butter them up to their faces so they would help him get elected and then curse them behind their backs.[37]

For a man who had taken the Hippocratic Oath, he was capable of alarming cruelty. Parks declared that she had seen him veer off the side of the road at seventy-five miles an hour in an effort to kill a dog. One of his favorite sayings was that he hated niggers, dogs, and Yankees, but in her estimation, he hated everybody.[38] He hated people who were in prison so much that he would give prisoners, particularly blacks, who had been locked up in solitary confinement a dose of castor oil. He relished the idea that the poor fellow who was locked up in a "tiny sweat box" would be forced to stand in his own excrement for several days.[39]

With the help of Hurston's vital insights, which she conveyed to him through numerous letters, Huie's investigation uncovered one shocking revelation after another. In an interview with the doctor's so-called closest friend, LaVergne Blue, Huie learned that Adams had been working on a sinister plot to defraud and possibly murder his friend. Blue owned a popular restaurant and cocktail lounge where Dr. Adams often ate with his friends and associates. LaVergne, who had no family, became close to Dr. Adams after the doctor made a house call to treat him for a viral lung infection. During those visits, Blue spent many hours with Adams at his bedside discussing the kind of personal and financial details of his life that one would only discuss with the closest of friends.[40]

A few weeks after Dr. Adams's funeral, LaVergne was informed that a copy of his last will and testament had been found in Dr. Adams's desk. This was puzzling, since LaVergne had never provided the doctor with a copy. When the will was turned over to LaVergne, he discovered that Dr. Adams had forged his name on the document, giving him all of LaVergne's property and total authority to dispose of the body.[41] There it was in black and white: indisputable evidence that Dr. Adams, the man who LaVergne had befriended and trusted with his life, had planned to defraud and possibly murder him and dispose of his body before an autopsy could be performed. Blue told Huie that Ruby must have realized that Adams was a monster before she killed him. He said that as far as he was concerned, Ruby had done the community a favor and that Suwannee County officials should commission a monument in her honor as a gesture of gratitude.[42]

Judge Adams made sure that Huie was never given the opportunity to talk to Ruby. But Huie won the draw when he revealed the results of his investigation in his best-selling book, *Ruby McCollum: Woman in the Suwannee County Jail*, which Hurston had originally hoped to collaborate on but later changed her mind about. Instead, she contributed an insightful thirteen-page commentary on her impressions of the trial (most of which had already been published in her *Courier* articles). Published in 1956, the book was so sensational that Huie would not allow his publishers to sell it in Florida for fear of possible lawsuits.

In addition to her contribution to his book, Hurston had hoped to collaborate with Huie on a literary piece called "The Cracker Crop." It was to be a collection of short stories, loaded with the colorful idiom of the southern cracker, about a hapless character named Cousin Mule who was always in trouble for "stealing mules, making love to widder woman, stealing good hound-dogs and lying magnificently."[43] Unfortunately, it never materialized.

In July 1954, two years before Huie's book was released, the Florida Supreme Court granted Ruby a new trial. But after eighteen months of incarceration, during which she claimed to have been forced to abort Adams's second child, Ruby's mental condition had deteriorated to the point where she was no longer competent to stand trial. As a result, she was committed to the state mental hospital in Chattahoochee, where she remained for twenty years. In 1974, she was released to her family in Ocala. She died a recluse at the age of 85 in May 1992.

6

A CRISIS IN DIXIE

Eau Gallie, 1954–1956

The whole matter revolves around the self respect of my people.
How much satisfaction can I get from a court order for somebody
to associate with me who does not wish me near them?

When the McCollum trial ended in late December 1952, Zora returned to her Eau Gallie farm and pondered her own fate. Just a few weeks shy of sixty-two, she was facing her golden years without the benefit of savings, investments, or dependable income. Her literary powers had dimmed with age and illness, and she was at odds with a racist and gender-biased publishing industry. She wrote constantly but published little and suffered from frequent bouts of gastric disorders and a hypertensive heart. Unsuccessful in her attempt to buy her Eau Gallie home, she scrambled to find the money "to grab a fine piece of property for almost nothing" located nearby.[1]

The property's owner, Thomas R. Barr, gave her until March 9, 1952, to come up with a $1,100 down payment on the eight-acre tract, which was uncleared but close to a highway. Still counting on the $800 she had been promised by the *Pittsburgh Courier*, she wrote her friend and former husband Herbert Sheen, now a Los Angeles physician, to ask him to loan her the rest: "You know very well that I would not ask this favor of you if things were not terribly pressing. I can see something really big coming from this land deal."[2] Not surprisingly, at least two well-established real estate companies shared her vision. The Harris-Van Bergen Group and the Gleason family's development firm were each champing at the bit, eager to make an offer if Hurston's deal fell through.[3] It was common knowledge that Eau Gallie and the neighboring city of Melbourne, which had been sleepy isolated areas for decades, were in the midst of a major economic transformation. Their close proximity to Patrick Air Force Base had resulted in a higher demand for housing and commercial development, turning available land in those areas into a hot commodity. An enthusiastic Hurston told Sheen, "One Yankee, Leveridge, has built (where there was nothing but weeds) about 600 new, modern houses (Leveridge Heights) and the new folks are taking the old settlers just like Grant took Richmond."[4]

Thomas Barr and his employer, Van Werley Land Development, Inc., were pushing Hurston to use the tract for a cheap Negro development, but she had other plans. Her intentions were to turn five acres into a commercial orange grove, lease two acres for a white trailer park, and use the rest for her home site. Given the success of Florida's citrus industry and the arrival of Cape Canaveral (Kennedy Space Center) in nearby Satellite Beach in the late 1950s, had Hurston been able to follow through on her plans, her life would have taken a decidedly different course. However, when the *Courier* failed to pay her the remaining $800 they owed her, she not only lost out on the land deal, she lost her car as well. Consequently, instead of reaping the benefits of a savvy investment, she spent the next few years working on her King Herod story, growing her own food, and scraping by on the money she earned from speaking engagements. She also earned a little income from her contribution to Huie's book and a short stint as a ghostwriter for a local white man.

In May, she granted an interview to reporter Leo Schumaker that appeared in the August 8, 1953, issue of *All-Florida Magazine*. The brief article, "Zora Hurston Sees King Herod Play As Her Greatest Work," included a photo of a slimmed-down, smiling, and confident Hurston wearing a black-and-white fitted dress. Schumaker praised her for her "infectious laughter" and "brilliant mind," which he characterized as "keenly alert to the fast moving events of today's world."

On December 14, 1953, Hurston was saddened to learn that Florida's literary legend, 57-year-old Marjorie Kinnan Rawlings, had died of a stroke. The two writers had been friends since the summer of 1942 when they were both living in St. Augustine, Florida. While completing her autobiography, Zora had taken a summer teaching position at St. Augustine's Florida Normal and Industrial College, where Rawlings was a frequent speaker.

Soon after they met, Rawlings invited Hurston to visit her and her husband Norton Baskin at their top-floor residence in Baskin's Castle Warden Hotel (now the location of Ripley's Believe It or Not Museum). Rawlings realized that seeing a black woman in her husband's whites-only hotel might upset his guests, so Baskin asked his colored bellhop to meet Zora in the hotel lobby and escort her to their quarters. When she failed to appear at the appointed time, he called his wife from his first-floor office and discovered that Hurston was already there.

Zora, being who she was, had also taken the delicate matter into consideration and thus avoided being seen by going through the kitchen and up the back stairs. When Rawlings answered her husband's call, she advised him to come on up and join the fun. During their visit, both Rawlings and Baskin fell head over heels for their dynamic guest. "She was the funniest thing you've ever seen, smart as could be too, he recalled."[5] Rawlings later described Zora as "a lush, fine-looking *café au lait* woman with the most ingratiating personality, a brilliant mind, and a fundamental wisdom that shames most whites."[6]

The admiration between Rawlings and Hurston was apparently mutual; the two writers came together for subsequent visits at Rawlings's Cross Creek home. After reading Rawlings's novel *Cross Creek*, Hurston praised her rich, authentic characterizations: "You have written the best thing on Negroes of any white writer who has ever lived. . . . You looked at them as they are, instead of slobbering over them as all of the other authors do. They talk real too, and act as I know them."[7] Rawlings returned the compliment in 1947, when she set up a meeting between Zora and her Scribner's editor, Maxwell Perkins, who had also worked with literary luminaries Scott Fitzgerald and Ernest Hemingway. By the end of their second meeting, Perkins had acquired a new client and Zora had walked away with not only an editor she considered to be the world's "brightest editorial light" but a new publisher and a $500 advance on her next book.[8] Unfortunately, Perkins died shortly after their meeting. He was replaced by Burroughs Mitchell.

The news of Rawlings's death sent Zora into a brief depression not only because of the loss but because she believed she had "failed her in her last extremity."[9] Rawlings had been among those friends who had stood by her through her darkest hours during the molestation investigation. When Rawlings wrote to Hurston earlier in the year to inform her of her illness, Zora had promised to come see her as soon as she could, but she never made the trip. "My car, like the old one-horse shay, just fell to pieces, and there I was with no transportation, and no means to replace it, and could not bear to admit it to her lest she feel sorry for me."[10] Now it was too late.

In the summer of 1955, telling Herbert Sheen that the time she had spent writing "Herod the Great" had constituted the "most formative years" of her life, Zora finally completed her last major literary undertaking and mailed it on to Mitchell who, much to her disappointment, found it unengaging: "In spite of your knowledge of your subject and your clearly deep feeling about it, the book does not seem to us to accomplish its intention. I mean to say that it does not vividly recreate the man and his time."[11] Although the story contained a great wealth of material, her editor felt that it failed to flow in a clear narrative stream, making it difficult for a layperson to understand. Robert Hemenway characterized its failings similarly, stating that the manuscript suffers from "poor characterization, pedantic scholarship, and inconsistent style."[12]

Zora took the rejection well, but she objected to what she interpreted as Mitchell's criticism of the lack of historical accuracy in her representation of the first century B.C.E. In response, Hurston expressed regret for his disappointment but defended her research: "My conclusion is this: It does not represent the accepted traditions of the period, but it does set forth the *facts*."[13] Furthermore, the history of the period that is generally accepted was distorted, she argued, by "more fables and fictions" sanctified by church tradition than can be imagined.[14] The rejection was a bitter blow, but she burned her disappointment like fuel and kept on going. Ever the optimist, Hurston wrote these words of encouragement to herself in a journal she kept for notes on Herod: "You are alive, aren't you? Well, so long as you have no grave you are covered by the sky. No limit to your possibilities. The distance to heaven is the same everywhere."[15] She never lost faith in the book's potential and continued to work on the manuscript with the hope that it would eventually be published.

In the spring of 1955, Hurston penned a moving memoir titled "The Enemy: A Unique Personal Experience" about the ravages of time (the enemy) and the alchemy of familial relationships. This poignant piece, which has received scant attention, recounts her friendship with a neighboring white family and their struggles with their 85-year-old matriarch after the death of her husband.

The family lived in a duplex apartment that was occupied by Mr. and Mrs. Pindar (Hurston recorded their names as Caldwell in a later version written in 1958) and their two children, seven-year-old Bobby and his eleven-year-old sister Helen, on one side. The other side was occupied by Mrs. Morris, the children's widowed grandmother, and her elderly parents Grandpa and Granny Brown.

Hurston's friendship with the family originated with the two Pindar children, who would often stop on their way home from school to play in the minnow pond behind Zora's cottage. "From halting to ask permission to play around the pond and watch the capers of the birds and the like," Hurston wrote, "we got to be very fond of each other and it kept up until the parents of the children came to know and like me too. It went on and on until we took to depending upon each other for small favors and things like that. Confiding and trustful."[16]

Zora had a special bond with little Bobby, who she described as a tender-hearted, imaginative, and "captivating child with heavy, curly dark hair, liquid dark eyes very thickly lashed, a graceful little body, and a winning grin."[17] Much like her own mother, who encouraged young Zora's storytelling, Hurston listened to Bobby with enthusiasm, knowing just the right places to be awed by his prowess as he spun his own tales about battling villains "with his fists and his arms curved upwards in the stylized manner of the current Western heroes."[18] She recalled, "Knighthood was in flaming flower with this handsome little boy."[19]

The Pindars and Mrs. Morris were the breadwinners of the family. Grandpa and Granny Brown lived on a small pension and kept a eye on their great-grandchildren while the Pindars were at work. This arrangement was particularly pleasing to Bobby, who idolized Grandpa Brown. "He would come home from school and rush next door to sit with the old couple and do little tasks and errands for them without complaint," Hurston recalled.[20] When the old man's health began to fail, he asked Bobby, who was proud and happy to have been chosen, to take care of Grandma Brown when he passed away, a promise that would later cause Bobby bewildering pain.

The family lived in harmony until the old man died. For months, Granny Brown had been getting around fine on her own, cooking and doing whatever was necessary to care for her ailing husband. However, as soon as the funeral was over, she removed her black mourning dress, "took to bed and resigned herself to helpless invalidism."[21]

Over the course of their long union, Grandpa Brown had catered to his wife's every whim. "It appeared that he had always treated her in this fashion since their marriage more than a half-century before," Hurston recalled.[22] "She would tell me with a smile how he had always babied and spoiled her."[23] Now that her beloved husband was gone, Granny Brown expected the rest of the family to follow his lead. Even if they had been willing, the Pindars and Mrs. Morris were too busy making a living to indulge the old woman. By the time Grandpa Brown died, mounting medical expenses had depleted his and his wife's savings, leaving the burdens of Granny Brown's care, her husband's funeral expenses, and a sizable medical bill to her daughter.

When the family failed to pamper her in the manner she had come to expect, the octogenarian became ever more helpless and demanding. As time went by, she refused to use her crutches to go to the bathroom, making it necessary to acquire a bedpan, and she continuously groaned until someone came to her bedside to keep her company. Although her daughter Mrs. Morris worked in a busy restaurant from five o'clock in the evening until one or two in the morning, the old woman expected her to get up at dawn to heed her beck and call. Hurston wrote, "Deprived of the petting she had received from her husband, she began to see the whole family as her enemy, especially her daughter, and set out to punish her for her 'crimes' of neglect. She took to screaming with pain around seven o'clock every morning . . . and would not desist until Mrs. Morris had been forced to get out of bed."[24]

Little Bobby did all that he could to fulfill his promise to take care of Granny Brown, but her demands proved more than he could handle. "It was only natural that he should become more and more reluctant as he was summoned from a sand lot ball game to sit beside his groaning Great-grandmother," Hurston observed.[25]

As the old woman's demands became increasingly unreasonable, the lives of her family grew more and more frazzled. Resentful that she was no longer the center of attention, Granny Brown "developed a fine technique in creating discomfort."[26] She would demand something to drink and then ignore it when it was brought to her. Likewise, she would beg for someone to fetch her bedpan five or six times an hour, then never use it.

In an effort to relieve their stress, the family asked Zora and other friends to sit with Grandma Brown for a few hours at a stretch. However, in need of a more permanent solution, the family eventually relocated the old woman to a nursing home. "Even the gallant Bobby felt relieved when she was moved and he was no longer required to abandon what pleased him to spend his working hours with her," Hurston recalled.[27] On Zora's subsequent visits to the nursing home, she was not surprised to find that the elderly Mrs. Brown had abandoned her helplessness and moaning and was walking on crutches, sitting in rocking chairs, and cheerfully conversing with the other residents.

Granny Brown was in the nursing home only a short time before she died. "I got the definite impression when I visited her there that she was a thwarted woman. The prey had escaped, and she had nothing to live for," Hurston opined.[28] While her passing was a relief for most of the family, it was a tragedy for little Bobby, who was wracked by guilt and grief.

While the adults were making funeral arrangements, Zora came over to watch the children. When Bobby saw her, he ran toward her, weeping, his fists balled up, trying to hit her as he yelled, "I hate you! . . . You let them take Granny to the old foks [sic] home."[29] Hurston caught his wrists and listened to him with understanding and compassion. To Bobby's young mind, it was all Zora's fault. She had known that Grandpa Brown had left Granny to his care and now she was dead. Exhausted with grief, the little boy finally rested his head on Zora's knee and "kept on sobbing with remorse and heartbreak."[30] When his pain was too great to bear, he would beat on her knee with his fist and blame her. Hurston recalled, "I kept telling him as gently as I knew how that he had nothing to blame himself for, but I knew that it would take at least twenty years to comprehend what I was saying. No use in my wasting time and effort then to try to make little Bobby aware of the sealing off of one generation from the other by time, so that the older ones become waste matter and slough off like the lower limbs of a pine."[31] Ultimately, Hurston wrote, "the real enemy was time. So I let him weep himself out and beat on my knee all he wanted to."[32]

Scribner's rejection of Hurston's Herod manuscript left her once again in dire financial straits. Having failed to secure a publishing contract, she sought out a book-finding service to help locate her out-of-print books, which she sold whenever possible as a means to generate income. She also pursued the possibility of having two of her books reprinted in Dutch. Some of her works had already been translated into French, Italian, Spanish, Swedish, German, Japanese, and Korean, and a Dutch translator named Madame Margrit De Sabloniere was working on Zora's behalf to persuade a publisher in Holland to produce a Dutch translation of either *Dust Tracks* or *Their Eyes* or both.

Hurston's attention was also focused on the social upheaval caused by the Supreme Court's landmark decision of 1954, *Brown v. Board of Education*, which ended segregation in public schools. She was not an advocate of segregation, but she opposed the decision, regarding the Court's insinuation that blacks needed to mix with whites in order to learn as an insult to her race. Moreover, Hurston considered a court order that forced races that had been segregated for centuries to suddenly mix as not only socially risky but an egregious abuse of the Court's power.

As a cultural anthropologist, folklorist, and writer, Hurston had devoted her life's work to demonstrating the esthetic, ideological, and social significance of black culture.[33] She held that the survival of African American culture and its traditions was central to the struggle against white dominance and racism.[34] To her mind, forcing black students to attend white educational institutions that excluded and devalued black culture robbed black children of traditions that contributed to their individual and cultural identities and self-esteem.[35] Like Senator Smathers, Hurston advocated a gradual rather than an immediate desegregation process.

She created an uproar the following summer when she made her views public in a provocative letter to the editor of the *Orlando Sentinel* that was published on August 11, 1955. Titled "Court Order Can't Make Races Mix," her letter posed the rhetorical question, "How much satisfaction can I get from a court order for somebody to associate with me who does not wish me near them?" She was appalled by what she deemed as the Court's insinuation that "there is no greater delight to Negroes than physical association with whites," a misconception that, she complained, the Communist Party exploited to enlist black members. With that in mind, she warned her readers that the Court's decree might be a harbinger of more "ominous" things to come: "What if it is contemplated to do away with the two-party system and arrive at government by decree? . . . Govt by fiat can replace the Constitution."

Bristling at the Court's implication that black teachers and institutions were inferior, she also took aim at what she perceived as the hypocrisy of the NAACP, arguing that "it is a contradiction in terms to scream race pride and equality while at the same time spurning Negro teachers and race association." Challenging the Court's resolve, she wrote:

If there are not adequate Negro schools in Florida, and there is some residual, some inherent and unchangeable quality in white schools, impossible to duplicate anywhere else, then I am the first to insist that Negro children of Florida be allowed to share this boon. But if there are adequate Negro schools and prepared instructors and instructions, then there is nothing different except the presence of white people. For this reason, I regard the ruling of the U.S. Supreme Court as insulting rather than honoring my race.[36]

Hurston's letter to the *Sentinel* sparked a raucous response from readers all over the country. Segregationists praised her for supporting their position and reinforcing white fear of miscegenation. Black leaders denounced her for her stubborn refusal to acknowledge the existing manifest inequalities between black and white schools, particularly in rural areas. Instead, she argued that "Negro schools in the state are in very good shape and on the improve."[37] Her position, which has been characterized by her critics as naive, shortsighted, and reactionary, earned her the reputation as a segregationist and a traitor to her race. And her friendships and support for conservative southern politicians Spencer Holland and George Smathers further fanned the flames.

Black public schools in Florida and throughout the South had suffered from impoverishment since 1896, when the Supreme Court's infamous "separate but equal" doctrine, which in practice meant "a little dab'll do you," made it easy and convenient to discriminate. Many black schools were housed in inferior and sometimes dilapidated buildings that had neither libraries nor laboratories, and while school buses were provided for white students, black children had none.[38]

Because taxes were the primary source of school funding, local governments, which were controlled by whites at every level, justified the minimal provisions for black schools by claiming that whites paid more taxes and should therefore have better schools. As late as 1940, $7.24 was allocated for every black child compared to $41.71 for every white child in Mississippi.[39] As a result of these inequalities, black principals were hired less for their qualifications and more for their ability to keep parents placated in the face of a deplorable lack of educational programs and progress. Black educators who had the courage to challenge the system were subjected to severe reprisals.[40]

However, Hurston's claim that Florida was making progress toward improving black education was essentially true. In the early 1940s, the Florida legislature made a significant stride toward the improvement of black schools, due primarily to the efforts of Dr. D. E. Williams of the State Department of Education. Under his leadership, the state approved the Minimum Foundation Public School Program with the intention of ending the practice of allowing communities to allocate minimal funding to black and poor white schools. Ideally, under this provision, all children in the state of Florida were assured a minimum standard of quality in their education through funding by the state. But the results of the program were mixed.

According to the Florida Department of Education, by 1952 Florida had closed the gap in capital outlays for new buildings for black schools by spending an average of $74.03 on white students and $79.18 on black students.[41] However, the inequality in expenditures per pupil, which paid for items such as books, equipment, and supplies, was not addressed. During the same year, white schools received $195.01 per pupil, while black schools received only $153.24.[42]

Although the rate of progress varied from state to state and from county to county, over the previous twelve years (1940–1952), the South had made significant gains in raising standards of public education to the national level. A report compiled by the U.S. Office of Education reported that the average per-pupil spending in southern schools in thirteen states had increased from $46.98 in 1940 to $163.00 in 1952.[43]

But while these increases were a sure sign of progress, the gap in per-pupil expenditures between black and white rural school districts was still substantial. Even after the passage of the Minimum Foundation Public School Program, Florida's white rural school districts received $189.51 per pupil in 1952, while its black counterparts received only $119.22 per pupil.[44]

But what Hurston certainly knew, and what modern research suggests, is that despite the material and fiscal inequalities within the public school system, the teachers and administrators of most African American schools had "made a way out of no way" in the development of nurturing, effective, and successful educational and socialization systems that reflected their culture and values.[45]

In his biography, Robert Hemenway argues that in her final years, Hurston became politically isolated and that her social and political views became too inflexible to "demonstrate a future vision."[46] While this observation holds some truth, it falls short in its analysis and characterization of Hurston's cultural sensibilities and the totality of her political thoughts and ideas during this time. For instance, Hurston's fear of the consequences of forced desegregation was not an isolated view but one that was shared by many Americans, black and white. In spite of her opposition to the *Brown* decision, Hurston enthusiastically shared the future vision of a desegregated America. Her main objection to the ruling was the method being used to achieve it.

Darwin Turner went even further, claiming that Hurston not only ignored the serious aspects of the lives of African Americans but also that she "inexplicably . . . denounced some of their efforts to secure equal opportunities in America."[47] Shibboleths often used to describe Hurston such as sellout, opportunist, and separatist clearly demonstrate that many of her political views are as contentious today as they were in her lifetime.

Given the monumental positive outcomes of the *Brown* decision regarding civil rights, it is easy to sympathize with Hurston's critics. There is no question that the historic decision set forth a continuing moral imperative and gave rise to the movement that ultimately led to the deconstruction of American apartheid. But to be fair, although Hurston failed to comprehend its ultimate political and social significance, some of her criticisms of the decision appear insightful and prophetic and reaffirm her social and political acumen, particularly when viewed through the lens of what we have learned about the effects of *Brown* in the last sixty years.

Based on case studies of segregated schools before *Brown*, researchers have discovered that African American schools across the South had established caring environments where every student was valued and encouraged to excel despite the obstacles put in place by a racist society.[48] These resources were vital to the success of their students. Additionally, as an integral part of the community, many African American schools were the epicenters of social, recreational, and cultural life at a time when few resources were provided for black communities.[49]

Contrary to what has been previously suggested, Hurston's concern for the loss of this vital cultural cohesion and her confidence in African American educational institutions were not isolated political views but were ones that were shared by many African Americans, including Rev. Dr. Martin Luther King, Jr. In 1959, in a candid conversation with two former black educators who had taught in the all-black Carver High School in Montgomery, Alabama, King expressed his concerns about the desegregation of public schools:

> I favor integration on buses and in all areas of public accommodation and travel. I am for equality. However, I think integration in our public schools is different. In that setting, you are dealing with one of the most important assets of an individual—the mind. White people view black people as inferior. A large percentage of them have a very low opinion of our race. People with such a low view of the black race cannot be given free rein and put in charge of the intellectual care and development of our boys and girls.[50]

Historical accounts and academic studies of the desegregation era demonstrate that many African American educators and parents shared King's concerns. When NAACP Legal Defense Fund representative Constance Baker Motley visited south Florida in 1954, she noted that some of the black teachers and administrators she met rejected integration in favor of equalization of facilities and resources, taking a "spend rather than blend" approach.[51]

In his classic article "Race and Education: A Search for Legitimacy," Harvard professor Charles V. Hamilton argues that before the *Brown* ruling, African Americans had every confidence in their capacity to educate their children. What they wanted was a fair share of the educational resources.[52] Unfortunately, as a result of southern resistance and a flawed implementation process, what they got in the short term were unfulfilled promises, hostility and violence, poor educational opportunities, the loss of thousands of black teachers and hundreds of black principals, and the eradication of their vital institutions and cultural traditions.

Because the Court's implementation decree did not require immediate compliance, southerners felt that they had been spared from a death sentence. The delay allowed them to organize legal resistance. Citizens' councils, refugees of the Ku Klux Klan, were organized to oppose any efforts toward desegregation, while southern governors sought legal grounds to challenge it.[53] Georgia and South Carolina refused to fund desegregated schools, forcing them to close. Alabama instituted a three-tier school system: one for blacks, one for whites, and one for those who chose to mix. Six other southern states enacted pupil assignment laws, giving school boards the power to assign white and black students to separate schools.[54] These tactics, which were designed to derail desegregation, were consistently upheld by district courts.

The steely defiance of southern resistance was best characterized in an editorial in the Richmond *News Leader* quoted by John Bartlow Martin in his book *The Deep South Says Never*: "Let us pledge ourselves to litigate this thing for fifty years. If one remedial law is ruled invalid, then let us try another; and if the second is ruled invalid, then let us enact a third."[55] In keeping with the *Leader*'s battle cry, from 1955 to 1957, southern legislatures enacted no fewer than 120 laws to oppose desegregation, which had in effect been outlawed by the Court's decision not only in public schools but in all public places.[56] In 1956, nearly every congressman in the Deep South, 101 in total, signed the "Southern Manifesto," a protest document that argued that the federal government had no power to force states to integrate schools. While legal battles and school boycotts were being staged, violence erupted across the South. Angry mobs blocked black children who tried to enter white public schools in Kentucky, where the National Guard was sent to restore law and order.[57]

These events, which Hurston described as "sickening," only strengthened her opposition to the Court's attempt to force revolutionary social change. Although she had been the first black student at Barnard College, she had been welcomed there, and she found it difficult to comprehend why Autherine Lucy, a black student who had been denied entrance into the all-white University of Alabama in 1952, would subject herself to public humiliation and threats of violence by fighting such discrimination through the courts, particularly when she had the option of attending quality African American colleges such as Tuskegee or Howard. "My nature would not permit me to go through what Authorine [sic] Lucy undertook. I could not bear to be so rejected. I am a sensitive soul and would rather go on to some school where I would be welcome."[58]

In a study conducted to determine the effects of desegregation in Tuscumbia County in Alabama, Vivian Gunn Morris and Curtis L. Morris reported that black students who were forced to attend white schools were met with hostility not only from the students but from the teachers and administrators as well.[59] These students also suffered academic losses when many southern white schools implemented a system known as "tracking." In this system, black students were relegated to lower-level classes and programs with the least amount of resources while their white counterparts were placed in well-funded accelerated or gifted classes and programs.[60]

These findings, which reflect the conclusion of similar studies conducted throughout the South, suggest that in addition to academic losses, one of the most damaging unintended consequences of *Brown* was the loss of the vital cultural connection and ethic of caring that had been bestowed on black students at their former all-black schools.[61] Sadly, by 1965, as a consequence of *Brown*, hundreds of black school principals and thousands of qualified, talented black teachers had been fired and hundreds of black schools had been closed. Despite these sacrifices, by the 1964–1965 school year, only 6.01 percent of black students in the eleven core southern states were attending school with whites.[62]

In 1971, when the Supreme Court ruled that lower courts had the authority to order busing of students from surrounding communities to achieve racial balance, white families who lived in urban school districts with court-ordered busing fled to the suburbs to avoid compliance. As a result, a pattern of segregated housing within cities emerged, leaving black students, who were shuffled in and out of white schools to take the places of white students who had fled, vulnerable to racial hostility and a curriculum that essentially ignored their needs.[63]

In 1954, when the *Brown* decision was announced, Derrick Bell, a former NAACP Legal Defense Fund attorney, believed with near-religious fervor that it was destined to be the "Holy Grail of racial justice."[64] However, in his book *Silent Covenant: Brown v. Board of Education and the Unfulfilled Hopes for Racial Reform* (2004), Bell, who had risked his life in support of *Brown*, contended that if he knew then what he knows now, he would have championed a different approach. He now argues that if the court had enforced "separate but equal" funding and resources for black schools during that period instead of forcing schools to desegregate, it might have been less contentious, less disruptive, and more effective: "In short, while the rhetoric of integration promised much, court orders to ensure that black youngsters actually received the education they needed to progress would have achieved more."[65] Others may argue that the sacrifices the black community made to achieve racial equality were an unavoidable and necessary consequence that gave momentum to the civil rights movement.

Regardless of where one stands on that issue, these testimonials and studies suggest what Hurston and others had tried to convey all along. While adequate funding and resources are vital to the operation of our educational systems, they are not the most important indicators of success. The conveyance of cultural values and traditions, the quality and commitment of caring educators and administrators, and the involvement of parents and the community all help determine the success of our students and schools.[66]

Ironically, despite the sacrifices, fifty-five years after *Brown*, significant racial and economic disparity in educational success and performance continues to be a challenge. Schools as well as communities all over the nation are steadily resegregating as dropout rates among minority students rise and achievement gaps widen. This unfortunate trend indicates that if America is to reaffirm *Brown*'s promise, there is still more work to be done.

The desegregation crisis was at an all-time high in the spring of 1956 when Sara Creech and her friend Elizabeth Sutton paid Hurston a visit. Sutton, a nationally recognized authority on the education of rural migrant children, had learned of Hurston through Creech and had asked her to introduce them. After making arrangements with Zora, the two women arrived at her Eau Gallie cottage around 1:30 on a lazy afternoon in March. Zora was still at church, so Creech and Sutton took a seat on the front porch swing and enjoyed the Indian River breeze while they awaited her return. Creech recalled, "The house and its surroundings were quaint and inviting. The walkway that led to her bright yellow cottage was lined with pink and purple flowers. When we approached the porch, two tabby-colored cats sleepily raised their heads to see who was coming."[67] The wide front porch was lined with an array of colorful flowerpots and, in addition to the swing, was furnished with two large white wicker rocking chairs. Next to the rockers, there was a rather small and worn-looking wooden writing table and chair that faced the lush wooded grounds.[68]

An earthy, exuberant Zora appeared a half an hour later in a floral print dress and wide-brimmed hat. After an effusive greeting, Zora apologized for her late appearance, explaining that when services had ended, the minister had sought her advice on ideas for a new radio program he was working on. Then she turned to Elizabeth and said, "Sara is such a good friend of mine that I feel that I already know you. *Her* friends are also *my* friends. And please, call me Zora."[69] With that said, the three women sat a long while as Zora and Elizabeth got better acquainted. Hurston talked breathlessly about her research on Herod, Creech touched on the recent activities of the interracial council, and Sutton described a pilot project she was supervising to educate migrant children in the Glades. When the subject of Negro education was broached, it inevitably led to a question about Hurston's controversial views.

Sutton, who was white, asked Zora why she objected to black children attending school with white children. Reaffirming her opposition to forcing students from vastly different cultural and socioeconomic backgrounds to mix in the classroom, her answer was swift and to the point: "In the first place, they cannot talk like white children; you cannot understand what they say. And, they are dirty. In fact, they stink!"[70]

According to Creech, Hurston never backed down from her position that black and white children in the South, particularly in the rural areas, were not ready for *Brown*. She was likewise convinced that the South in general was not yet ready to embrace wholesale integration. There were exceptions, she conceded, herself included. But otherwise, she told her guests, "We have to earn our places, and I want you to know that I have been a guest in many white homes. In fact, I can go into any home I choose to visit."[71] In response, Creech replied, "That's because you are such an interesting person that you transcend race. You have an unusual body of knowledge and can challenge any of us on practically any subject."[72]

With that said, the topic was put aside and Zora offered her guests some refreshments. After disappearing through the front door, she returned a few minutes later with traditional southern refreshments: a tray of sugar cookies and a pitcher of homemade lemonade. While they enjoyed the treats, Zora regaled her guests at Sutton's request, as she had done countless times to audiences all over the country, with a fascinating account of her research and experiences in Haiti and Jamaica. Sadly, this memorable two-hour visit was the last time Creech saw Zora before Hurston's death in 1960.

Shortly after their visit, Zora got word that her beloved Eau Gallie home, where she had spent some of the happiest years of her life, had been sold. Now she faced the prospect of starting over once again. She briefly considered moving back to Miami and tried, to no avail, to arrange a European folk concert tour. On May 28, 1956, she attended a commencement ceremony as a special podium guest at Bethune-Cookman College in Daytona Beach, where she had briefly taught dramatics in 1934. During the ceremony, she was honored with an award from the college for her outstanding contributions to education and human relations.

The middle of the decade bought Hurston other recognition as well. In addition to the letters she received from folks all over the country commending her for her dramatic and literary contributions, both Hoyt Fuller, a magazine editor, and Richard Bardolph, a North Carolina professor, planned to include her profile in their articles on black women authors. And she often received letters asking permission to excerpt and anthologize her work.[73]

After considering her options, she decided to accept a position as librarian at the Technical Library for Pan American World Airways, Inc., located twenty miles north at Patrick Air Force Base. The job was relatively easy, and it would provide her with steady income at $325 per month. To ready herself for the move, she found homes for her dog's puppy and her numerous cats and purchased a station wagon she dubbed "the truck." After securing an efficiency apartment, she packed up her belongings and moved on to her new life in Cocoa Beach.

1

THE LAST HORIZON

Fort Pierce, 1956–1960

*I feel that I have lived. I have had the joy and pain of strong
friendships. . . . I have loved unselfishly . . . and I have hated with
all the power of my soul. . . . I have touched the four corners of the
Horizon, for from hard searching it seems to me that tears and
laughter, love and hate, makeup the sum of Life.*

Hurston began her new job on June 18, 1956.[1] Her duties managing
Pan American's technical literature were relatively easy and the posi-
tion provided her with a steady income. In April, finding her Cocoa
Beach efficiency apartment at 516½ King Street inadequate, she rented
a comfortable, private mobile home eleven miles from Patrick AFB
on Merritt Island, located across the Indian River. There, as always,
Hurston made friends with her neighbors. One of her friends, Daisy
Tucker, recalls, "We went to the drive-in movie. They had a 'whites
Only' rest room. Zora said she was going to the rest room. I said, 'You
can't; that's for whites only.' She said, 'I'm going,' and she did go. She
didn't integrate the rest room, she commandeered it!"[2]

But just as her living arrangements improved, in seesaw-like fashion, her job situation worsened. After only a few weeks on the job,
she was thrust into a heated controversy over the firing of fellow employee Eva Lynd, who had reported a male supervisor for destroying
classified documents without following proper security procedures.
After an investigation of the matter led to the supervisor's termination, Hurston praised Lynd's actions as an act of patriotism, but
the rank and file considered her a stool pigeon and an outcast. When

Lynd was later fired under questionable circumstances, Hurston was furious.

The growing chasm between Zora and other members of the library staff, who she referred to as "latter-day carpetbaggers," was further widened by what she perceived as their condescension toward southerners.[3] The irony of this perception was particularly vexing since she was better educated and more accomplished than anyone there. Hurston's frequent complaints of boredom, her objection to the hiring of undereducated personnel, and her opposition to Lynd's firing led to months of what she characterized as "sadistic persecution" and ultimately ended with her termination on May 10, 1957.[4] Obviously intended for optimum sarcasm, the reason for Zora's termination department head William McKay gave was that she was "too well-educated for the job."[5] She was so furious, she wrote to Vice President Richard Nixon to protest her termination as a violation of the Fair Employment Practices Act.[6]

When her position at the library ended, she remained in the area for several months receiving unemployment, booking speaking engagements, corresponding with friends, and revising her "Herod the Great" manuscript. Turning her attention once again to the issue of desegregation and southern politics, she told her friend Mary Holland that she planned to write an article on Holland's husband titled "Take For Instance Spessard Holland" for the *Saturday Evening Post* that focused on the plight of the southern lawmaker. "The general impress[i]on of the North is that a Southern Senator is a lay figure, activated only by racial stimuli. I yearn to show the inevitable prolonged thought, speculation and pondering in the mind of a cultivated man like Spessard L. Holland," she declared.[7] (The article was never published.)

Zora had been a friend and supporter of Senator Holland and his wife since their meeting in the early 1940s when he was Florida's twenty-eighth governor. In addition to reforming the state tax system, Governor Holland had been a strong advocate of public education. During his four-year term (1941–1945), he supported legislation to increase funding to public schools, create a teacher retirement system, and raise teachers' salaries.[8] As a U.S. senator, serving from 1946 to 1971, he was adamantly opposed to desegregation by judicial decree and signed the infamous "Southern Manifesto" in protest.[9] Although he opposed forced desegregation, he, like Smathers, was one of the few southern politicians who openly invited his black friends and acquaintances to his home. He also supported the right of black citizens to vote and in 1964 voted to eliminate Florida's poll tax.[10]

Hurston interpreted Senator Holland's opposition to the *Brown* decision as a genuine concern for race relations in the South. He believed, as did Hurston, that federally forced integration was a mistake, preferring a state-led effort to encourage gradual change instead. As governor of Florida, he took an alternative approach to the race issue: "He began at the only realistic place to begin, the foundation, by stepping up the educational program among us. He is of the Herbert Hoover type, sticks to fundamentals and leaves the flashy gestures to the demagogues," Hurston wrote.[11]

Hurston blamed the NAACP, President Dwight D. Eisenhower, and the *Brown* decision for what she perceived as the "hate-filled, stinking mess" in which southern blacks and whites found themselves.[12] She surmised that the NAACP was "quite annoyed" with her for insisting that they were "working on the wrong end of the Negro," referring to the bus boycotts (which were being led by an upstart civil rights leader named Martin Luther King, Jr.) and sit-ins taking place in Florida and all over the South.[13] Expounding on Booker T. Washington's philosophy of self-determination, she argued that "all their fights boil down to a matter of *seats*. Knowing conditions as I do, I clamor that improvements should start on the other end. . . . Let us not concern ourselves so much about wheve [sic] we are going to sit, but rather what we are going to DO to contribute to the welfare of this nation. Be givers and not receivers only." Confident in her opinion, she added, "That is the only answer, and eventually we will be driven to it whether we will or not."[14]

While the future of race relations in the South remained uncertain, Hurston remained stalwartly optimistic about her own future despite her declining health, her financial hardship, and repeated rejections from publishers. Believing that her work on King Herod had brought her to the pinnacle of her abilities, in June she revealed a profound confidence and inner satisfaction in a letter to Herbert Sheen: "As for myself, I have gone through a period that might appear outwardly unprofitable, but in reality extremely important. . . . I feel that I have made phenomenal growth as a creative artist."[15]

Looking backward, she expressed pride in her lifelong artistic and scholarly achievements: "I am not materialistic. I do take a certain satisfaction in knowing that my writings are used in many of the great universities both here and abroad, both literary and anthropological. If I do happen to die without money, somebody will bury me, though I do not wish it to be that way."[16]

Hurston had every right to be proud of her accomplishments. But for all she had been and done, at age sixty-six, when financial security is imperative, she was penniless and jobless, weakened by a gastric ailment, and suffering from advancing heart decease (exacerbated by many years of cigarette smoking). And though her anthropological and literary works were in fact being used in some of the most prominent universities in the United States and abroad, none of those institutions had offered her a teaching post.

At the end of 1957, Hurston's economic picture brightened when C. E. Bolen, the owner of a black weekly newspaper, offered her a part-time job as a columnist for his Fort Pierce–based paper, the *Chronicle*. Without hesitation she accepted the position, packed her belongings for the last time, and moved eighty miles south to Fort Pierce to live out the remaining years of her life.

Located along the banks of the beautiful Indian River, Fort Pierce proved to be a haven. After spending a lifetime challenging the status quo, staving off poverty, and beating the odds, Hurston embraced all the things that the community gladly provided: employment, friendship, comfort, compassion, stability, and, above all, love and respect.

Zora formed several close friendships during this period, but her most ardent admirer and friend was Dr. C. C. Benton, a black physician who had grown up near Eatonville and had been acquainted with

Zora's father and some of her brothers. After hearing about her financial difficulties, the kindly gray-haired physician generously waived the $40 monthly rent she was paying on the small green cement cottage he owned at 1734 School Court. He also served as her attending physician. Recognizing Hurston for the extraordinary human being that she was, Dr. Benton and his two daughters, Arlena and Margaret, extended to Zora the kind of deference and affection usually reserved for a beloved matriarch. A handsome, well-informed, educated man, Dr. Benton would often close his medical office early to drop by Hurston's cottage for a few hours of intelligent conversation and lively debate. Some of their conversations were so profound that the doctor admits, "She lost me."[17] He filled her cupboards with food, tended to her health, and dutifully picked her up every Sunday to have dinner with his family.

According to Benton's nurse, Helen Barr, the good doctor would often have several Sunday dinner guests in addition to Zora. When the meal was over, they would engage in conversation or head over to the Elks Club to take in a performance by local musicians.[18] Art Johnson, who was then a teenager, remembers one such occasion when Hurston, Benton, and his guests came to hear his band. "I didn't realize who Zora was at the time, but I remember that she really enjoyed herself."[19]

Zora also enjoyed the bohemian atmosphere and jazz sessions at the home of A. E. "Beanie" Backus, a celebrated local white landscape painter. A native of Fort Pierce, Backus was known as the "Dean of the Florida Landscape," for no other twentieth-century painter captured the beauty of Florida light as brilliantly. Backus is also credited with launching a now-famous group of black landscape painters known as the Highwaymen through his mentoring of their revered founder, Alfred Hair.

In addition to her friends in the arts, Zora kept company with two local white journalists, Marjorie Silver Alder and Ann Wilder, who often joined her at the gatherings at the Backus house. Ann Wilder was a reporter for the *Miami Herald*. Marjorie and her husband Doug had moved to Fort Pierce from New York City, where she had been a writer for the soap opera *Little Sister* and he had been a public relations professional. After moving to the area, the couple bought a local radio station and became politically active; Marjorie was the first female to be elected to the St. Lucie County Commission.

Marjorie met Zora after receiving a call from an employment service representative who said that there was a black writer in town who was in need of a friend.[20] While living in New York, Marjorie had heard about Zora and read her books and was an admirer. As soon as Hurston called, she invited her over to her riverfront home. "The first afternoon Zora came over, was like she was digging in an archaeological site for something. After that, she blossomed out and was Zora," Alder recalled.[21] From that point on, Zora was a frequent visitor and guest in Alder's home and at her dinner parties, for which she sometimes arrived wearing colorful exotic clothing and a turban. After dinner, it was her custom to bring home the leftovers to feed to the neighborhood children while telling them stories and encouraging them to be proud of their African American heritage.[22]

Zora's cottage was small but comfortable. In addition to a living area, bathroom, and kitchen, it had two small bedrooms. The terrazzo floors were covered with colorful throw rugs and the living room was furnished with overstuffed beanbag chairs, a table, and a lamp. She had a small kerosene stove in the kitchenette for preparing meals, a trunk in which she kept her papers and manuscripts, and a small dressing table and bed. She lived as frugally as possible, converting wooden fruit crates into bookshelves and a writing table. As she had in Eau Gallie, she planted a vegetable and flower garden.[23]

Using her abundance of rich materials, Hurston wrote for the *Chronicle* from 1957 to 1959. Her writings included a weekly column called "Hoodoo and Black Magic" as well as pieces on the Indian River, race relations, and Florida's cultural history. Two of her articles, published on February 6, 1959, included "The Tripson Story," about the amazing skills of Eddie Darrisaw, a cowboy who worked at the Tripson Dairy, and a piece on the Sexton family's Treasure Hammock Ranch, both located in nearby Vero Beach. And, as always, she continued her work on Herod. When she wasn't writing, she enjoyed her favorite pastimes: fishing in the Indian River and reading everything from humorous to serious works.

In February 1958, she accepted a position as an English teacher at Lincoln Park Academy, a local black high school, with the understanding that the school would assist her in obtaining a valid Florida teaching certificate. The school, founded in 1914, boasted a population of 329 students and had earned a reputation for excellence. Hurston, though, was soon disillusioned, complaining that despite its good reputation, the school was plagued with undisciplined, knife-carrying, dice-toting, over-school-age male students and that her homeroom was purported to be the worst on campus.

But Shirley Crawford, one of Zora's English students, remembers it differently. "As a teacher, Zora was probably more aware of things like that than I was, but I don't recall a lot of discipline problems at the school. There were about twenty students in a class and the new principal, Leroy C. Floyd, a strict disciplinarian, was proud of the school and did not tolerate misbehavior."[24] Crawford believes that Zora had difficulties with some of the students largely because they regarded her as a substitute teacher. She had replaced another instructor, James C. Jenkins, who had been discharged in the middle of the term after being arrested for drunkenness and for pointing a gun at another man and threatening to kill him. Her unconventional style of dress, including colorful skirts and blouses and big hats, generated nasty comments and gestures by some of her less sensitive students when her back was turned.

Though she may have dressed funny, Crawford and others, such as former student Marjorie Harrell, were intrigued by Hurston's teaching style. "Instead of using a textbook, she incorporated her grammar lessons with stories and fables about life. None of her students knew how famous Zora was, but they enjoyed her class. She would read stories from what I now realize were her own books, with great dramatic flair," Harrell recalls.[25] Hurston also encouraged students whom she believed had talent. One such student was Georgia Porter, who Zora recommended to C. E. Bolen to work as an intern for the *Chronicle*.[26]

Cleo Leathe, a Lincoln Park Academy social studies teacher, admired Zora's dedication: "It was obvious that her health was failing, but she came to school every day and gave it her all."[27] Once when they walked together to a school pep rally, Zora complained about the school taking twelve minutes from each academic class in order to make time for the rally, which she considered frivolous.

The assembly schedule was one among many things that Hurston found irksome. She also wanted to do away with the school's corporal punishment policy, revamp the English curriculum, and replace some of its teaching methods with techniques she had mastered as a folklorist. Having found that blacks were "predominantly aural-minded," she believed that schools needed to devise a better and faster means of teaching black children. After all, she reasoned, "intelligence measurements rest on the quantity and the quality of attention."[28] She also took issue with the school's disciplinary policy regarding corporal punishment. Her view was that it was not an effective means of promoting decent behavior. In its place, she advocated the use of "reasoning," particularly since most of her overage and hardened students had become accustomed to violence as a way of life. And besides, once they arrived at a certain age and physical size, corporal punishment was no longer appropriate.[29]

Most of Hurston's colleagues considered her an odd bird, but she enjoyed good relationships with Leathe and her *Chronicle* boss Bolen, who was also the school's physical education director. Zora believed that her failure to connect with other colleagues was due to jealousy. "My name as an author is too big to be tolerated, lest it gather to itself the 'glory' of the school here. . . . They feel invaded and defeated by the presence of creative folk among them," she surmised.[30]

In the beginning of March, her brief stint as an English teacher came to a halt. Although she had applied for a teaching certificate with the state Department of Education, and had been assured that it would be forthcoming as soon as the department received her Barnard

College transcript, Principal Floyd was unwilling to wait. Instead, on March 10, he dismissed her from her teaching post.

Given the relative certainty of her certification, Zora suspected that she had been fired for, among other things, insubordination. In a letter to Mitchell Ferguson, a coordinator for the state Department of Education, Hurston stated that she believed she was dismissed because of jealousy on the part of her colleagues and her disagreement with the administration over corporal punishment: "I admit that I have not resorted to their methods because it is a sad fact that Negroes are given too much violence."[31]

Contrary to Hurston's assumptions, the delay in obtaining her teaching certificate was most likely the primary reason for her termination. According to scholar Gordon Patterson, in February 1958, the same month Hurston was hired, Floyd was in the midst of preparing Lincoln Park Academy's self-evaluation before a visit from the Southern Association of Colleges and Secondary Schools for the purpose of school accreditation.[32] One of the requirements for accreditation is that all faculty members have proper state certification. While her overt criticisms of the school likely worsened matters, it is possible that Lloyd was forced to let Zora go lest the school be cited for noncompliance.

Once again in need of support, Hurston turned to her writing. Hoping to sell a series of stories on migrant labor camps in Florida, Hurston took Marjorie Silver Alder's advice to pitch the idea to George Beebe, an editor for the *Miami Herald*. Beebe responded positively, but when the first installment arrived, he and his editors were unimpressed. In a letter to Doug Silver, Beebe explained that the piece lacked a unifying purpose and that he wondered, given Hurston's literary reputation, whether she had engaged a ghostwriter to help her write her previous articles for national magazines.[33]

After the *Herald*'s rejection, Zora turned to her passion, Herod the Great. Having revised and polished her manuscript for five long years, she was now eager to find a publisher. Scriber's Sons had declined the manuscript in 1955, and she had drifted away from her former publisher, J. B. Lippincott. Hurston sent her revised manuscript to the small upstart David McKay Publishing Company. But much to her disappointment, they too declined the work.

Suffering from worsening health, Zora was admitted to Fort Pierce Memorial Hospital on September 19 for hypertensive heart disease, brought on by prolonged high blood pressure, excessive weight (she weighed around 200 pounds), and nicotine addiction. A month later, she downplayed the seriousness of her illness in a high-spirited letter to friend Sara Creech. Casting her eyes toward the future, Hurston told Creech that she was soon to acquire a small plot of land where she hoped to grow greens for local florists. In the meantime, she had enlisted the help of the black community as well as the Fort Pierce mayor and city manager "to set up what I call a DO-IT-YOURSELF playground for Negroes in which we choose the type of games we want, then somehow get the equipment ourselves."[34] Her next endeavor was to ask former Brooklyn Dodger Roy Campanella, one of professional baseball's beloved African American pioneers, to come to Fort Pierce to inspire its youth. After that, she told Creech, she was going to "keep right on advocating personal initiative till I am bombed out."[35]

Still hoping to find a publisher for "Herod," in the summer of 1959, Hurston turned to Marjorie Silver Alder for help. At the time, Marjorie was conducting a syndicated radio program that required regular trips to New York. At Hurston's behest, she agreed to take a few chapters of the manuscript with her to distribute to various New York publishing houses.[36] After reading the chapters herself, Alder experienced a sad revelation. "It wasn't her," she said.[37] However, having made Zora a promise, she dutifully submitted the chapters to three publishers for possible publication. They all declined.

Zora's last known letter was written on January 16, 1959, a week after her sixty-eighth birthday. Ever hopeful of selling "Herod," she wrote a letter to Harper Brothers asking if they would have any interest in it: "One reason I approach you is because you will realize that any publisher who offers a life of Herod as it really was, and naturally different from the groundless legends which have been built up around his name has to have courage."[38] Sadly, after devoting many years researching and writing about Herod, Hurston's self-proclaimed masterpiece was never published.

Because of her deteriorating health, Hurston was no longer able to write articles for the *Chronicle*. Having no means of support, she applied for welfare and food stamps. Dr. Benton provided anything else she needed. As proud as ever, she continued to live alone, refusing to let her family know the financial and physical difficulties she was facing until October 12, when she suffered a stroke and was hospitalized. She remained in the hospital until October 29 and was then transferred to the segregated Lincoln Park Nursing home, operated by the St. Lucie County Welfare Agency. It was a hard transition for Hurston, who had taken such enormous pride in her independence, but the stroke had weakened her cognitive powers and rendered her unable to care for herself.

In addition to the Benton family, Marjorie Silver Alder, and Ann Wilder, Hurston was visited by others who loved her, including her brother Clifford Joel, his wife Mabel, and their daughter Vivian. But when Clifford tried to give Zora money and buy her some things he thought she needed, she refused it all. Friend Ann Wilder remembers that Zora's room in the basement was a rather gloomy, dreary place. Zora was conscious, but her stroke had left her unable to communicate. "To stimulate her mind and help her pass the time, I used to sit with her and tell her all about the news from around the community," Wilder recalled.[39] "Even though she was on the down track, you didn't really feel sorry for her, because she knew who she was, and that she might have to be on charity, but she knew her quality." And thinking back on Zora's spirit, she added, "It wasn't exactly pride, it was an inner self-confidence that never failed her."[40]

To use Hurston's colorful phrasing, after suffering a second stroke, "Old Death" with his "soft feet" tiptoed into Zora's room on January 29, 1960, just after sundown. Within days of her passing, just three weeks after her sixty-ninth birthday, Marjorie Silver Alder and Margaret Paige of Lincoln Park Academy began efforts to raise money to give Zora a decent burial. To get the word out, Alder wrote an article about

Hurston for the *Miami Herald* that was picked up by the wire services and published in major newspapers around the country.

Soon after, independent obituaries, including those in the *New York Times* and *Time* magazine, began to appear. Within days, Percy S. Peek's Funeral Home, which had donated the plot, received a total of $661.87 to pay for what the *Chronicle* described as "one of the nicest funerals ever in the St. Lucie County area."[41] Both J. B. Lippincott and Scribner's Sons sent a donation of $100, and the small funeral home on Avenue D in Fort Pierce also received checks from Fannie Hurst and Carl Van Vechten. Former colleagues at Lincoln Park Academy and Zora's former students also contributed to the effort.

The funeral rites were held at Peek's Funeral Chapel on Sunday, February 7, 1960, at three o'clock. There were so many attendees that Curtis Johnson, the funeral director, had to extend the seating to the sidewalk. By all accounts, there were more than 100, including her brothers John and Clifford and Clifford's wife Mabel. At least sixteen whites, including Sara Creech, Beanie Backus, Marjorie Silver Alder, Doug Silver, Ann Wilder, and Florida author Theodore Pratt, also attended the hour-long service.[42]

Creech and others who attended the funeral service recalled that Zora was laid out in a frilly pink dressing gown. The flower arrangements, which came from all over the country, were so numerous that they almost obscured her white-and-pink steel casket. The ceremony began with a processional ("Nearer, My God to Thee"), a prayer offered by Rev. H. W. White, and a reading from scripture by Rev. R. J. Cliffin. Mrs. L. W. Halbe and Betty Williams sang beautiful solos, and the Lincoln Park Academy Chorus also performed. After remarks from C. E. Bolen and Leroy Floyd, Rev. W. A. Jennings, Sr., delivered the eulogy.

In his eulogy Rev. Jennings stated: "They said she couldn't become a writer recognized by the world. But she did it. The Miami paper said she died poor. But she died rich. She did something."[43]

After the service, six pallbearers carried Hurston's casket out of the funeral home, followed by a retinue of nine Lincoln Park Academy flower girls. She was taken to the city's segregated cemetery, the

Genesee Memorial Gardens (Sarah's Memorial Garden), to be buried. Before Hurston's interment, Theodore Pratt delivered a moving graveside tribute, calling her "a prime example of the excellent American writer who, in our smash-hit or virtually nothing kind of literary civilization, gets lost in the shuffle." Lamenting this injustice, he further declared, "Far more recognition should be given to such writers, and I ask permission to give this to Zora."[44] Expressing similar sentiments, Hurston's lifelong friend Carl Van Vechten wrote, "I LOVED Zora and want her memory kept green."[45]

Fannie Hurst also paid tribute to her friend and former travel companion. In her article, "Zora Neale Hurston: A Personality Sketch," published in Yale University's *Library Gazette*, Hurst described Zora as "a gift to both her race and the human race." Praising Zora in terms that made Van Vechten weep, Hurst wrote, "To life, to her people, she left a bequest of good writing and the memory of an iridescent personality of many colors. Her short shelf of writings deserve[s] to endure. Undoubtably [*sic*], her memory will in the minds and hearts of her friends. We rejoice that she passed this way so brightly, but alas, too briefly."[46]

If Pratt, Van Vechten, and Hurst were alive today, they and all of Hurston's contemporary admirers would be gratified to know that just as her editor Burroughs Mitchell predicted shortly after her death, Zora and her works were eventually rediscovered. Never mind that she died with her books out of print and was buried in an unmarked grave, Hurston and her literary contributions were destined to be central to the canon of African American, American, and women's literatures.

The efforts to preserve Hurston's legacy began with a Fort Pierce deputy sheriff named Patrick Duval. Soon after her death, Duval was riding past Hurston's former cottage when he noticed a fire in the backyard. When he stopped to investigate, he discovered that the crew that had been hired to clean out the cottage was burning the contents of Hurston's storage trunk. Having known Zora and the value of her material, he quickly grabbed the water hose and put the fire out.[47] The badly charred contents, which included correspondence, documents, various writings, and Hurston's "Herod the Great" manuscript, were donated to the Department of Rare Books and Manuscripts at the University of Florida in Gainesville.

Since that time, after decades of obscurity, Hurston and her works have enjoyed a resurgence in popularity. Her books, which are now printed in English, Spanish, French, Italian, German, Japanese, and Dutch, continue to enjoy brisk sales. In 2005, her wildly popular novel *Their Eyes Were Watching God* was introduced to millions of viewers when Oprah Winfrey released her film version starring Halle Berry and Ruby Dee. Having been recognized for her literary genius, Hurston is currently the subject of college courses and dissertations, anthologies, books, critical essays, literary seminars, biographies, bibliographies, children's literature, documentaries, and plays. After a successful debut on Broadway in 1991, her folk comedy *Mule Bone* is being produced by professional and community theaters throughout the country, as is her play *Polk County*.

As an icon of racial pride and uncompromising fortitude, she has inspired a generation of female African American writers as well as readers and writers, both male and female, of all races around the world. In addition to two annual Florida festivals held in her honor—one in Eatonville and another in Fort Pierce—Hurston has had numerous museums, libraries, schools, and government buildings named for her.

Those who knew and loved Zora Neale Hurston during her lifetime need not have worried. Her life, her achievements, and her body of work have transcended race and time and have given us the gift of an enduring legacy.

CONCLUSION

Hurston lived the last decade of her life the same way she had always lived it, with courage, resilience, generosity, and aplomb. Her last years were fraught with ill health, financial difficulties, and personal and professional disappointments, yet she maintained an unrelenting joie de vivre. Her ability "to come out more than conquer"[1] helped her survive devastating morals charges, the libelous reporting of the black press, and a personal vendetta to destroy her career. However, the experiences left their scars.

Stung by betrayal, by the time she returned to Florida in 1950, she had become disgruntled with the members of her race. In a letter to William Bradford Huie, she wrote: "I want no parts of them, and if somebody were to set up a nation of American Negroes, I would be the very first person NOT to go there."[2] Over time her wounds healed, but she remained distrustful.

Disappointed though she was, Hurston never lost her characteristic zeal for black culture. She continued to promote its esthetic, social, and cultural significance in her writings, her concerts, and her work with the Belle Glade Inter-Racial Council and through her vital support and promotion of Creech's Saralee doll. In her article "What White Publishers Won't Print" (1950) she challenged whites' stereotypical images of African Americans and other minorities and lambasted white publishers for their lack of courage to publish material that dispelled those myths.

The Cold War and the racial politics of the era reaffirmed her social and political philosophies and her uncompromising anti-communist position, both of which were manifest in her political commentaries, including "Why Negroes Won't Buy Communism" (1951) and "Court Order Can't Make Races Mix" (1955). Her abhorrence of communism, which peaked during the Joseph McCarthy hearings, was in line with that of many Americans. But her belief in the power of individualism as the primary means of racial uplift and her resistance to collective action as a means to promote social change put her at odds with the strategies of the NAACP and its supporters. In her article "Crazy for This Democracy" (1945), Hurston called for the end of Jim Crow "now and forever!"[3] However, her opposition to the *Brown* decision nine years later and her failure to support the organized resistance that led to the civil rights movement resulted in widespread criticism that continues today.

While some of Hurston's philosophies may have been eccentric and out of sync with the mainstream beliefs of her contemporaries, it is important to note that she nonetheless possessed the cultural, social, and political sensibilities to accurately anticipate *Brown*'s failings, an observation for which she is seldom credited.

In her coverage of the Ruby McCollum trial, Hurston confronted political corruption, injustice, race, and gender discrimination head on. Ultimately, with the help of friend William Bradford Huie, she exposed the highly charged political force that silenced the truth and robbed McCollum of her right to justice.

Although none of her novels completed during the 1950s were published, they stand as testaments to her courage and determination to push the literary envelope. As John Lowe observes, "She altered the terms of black-white literary discourse, for she accepted the modernist shift in stance from a presentation aimed at sincerity to one that expressed authenticity."[4] Just as she had done with *Their Eyes*, "The Golden Bench of God" was a valiant effort to continue to break through the cultural and literary barriers that had limited the focus and development of black literature. Through diligence and sacrifice, Hurston paved the way for black women to write about their inner lives and have such work taken seriously.

Hurston's writing on Herod represents one of the first challenges to the accepted wisdom surrounding Herod's life and career. According to the listings of the Library of Congress, until 1956, when British biographer Stewart Perowne published *The Life and Times of Herod*, in which he too challenged the credibility of Josephus's writings, the only definitive modern scholarship on Herod was in *History of the Jewish People in the Time of Christ* by German theologian Emil Schurer (1886).[5] Today, as a result of modern scientific archaeology and scholarship, Hurston's challenges to the historical accuracy of the writings of Josephus and Matthew have been validated and expanded and continue to fuel lively scholarly debate.

Hurston passionately wanted her books published, but it was the writing, the work itself, that was most vital to her. As a creative artist, she reinvented her style and modes of narration in response to her varying subjects and interests.[6] As long as she was working, she was content. In *Dust Tracks*, she wrote, "I don't know anymore about the future than you do. I hope that it will be full of work, because I have come to know by experience that work is the nearest thing to happiness that I can find. No matter what else I have among the things that humans want, I go to pieces in a short while if I do not work."[7]

In addition to her writing, Hurston was sustained by her correspondence and relationships with friends and family. According to Carla Kaplan's *Zora Neale Hurston: A Life in Letters*, from 1950 until her death she wrote a total of eighty-four known letters, telegrams, and postcards. In *Dust Tracks* she wrote: "Without the juice of friendship, I would not be even what I seem to be. So many people have stretched out their hands and helped me along my wander. With the eye of faith, some have beheld me at Hell's dark door, with no rudder in my hand, and no light in my heart, and steered me to a peace within."[8] Hurston continued to cherish and nurture her old friendships while forging new ones throughout her life. In addition to the Creech family and the friends she made in Miami, Belle Glade, Eau Gallie, and Fort Pierce,

Hurston remained close to her former husband Herbert Sheen, her dear friend Carl Van Vechten, and her remaining family members, particularly her brothers Everett and John and their families.

As an ancestral spirit, Hurston's life and works continue to move and inspire us. In addition to her remarkable literary achievements and irrepressible spirit, she will be remembered as a person who lived her life on her own terms, a life fully realized, a life graced with deep love and friendship, a life that pushed, prodded, challenged, and celebrated without (as she would put it) "ringing no backing bells."

ACKNOWLEDGMENTS

The completion of this book would not have been possible without the generous assistance, contributions and support of numerous librarians, scholars, colleagues, friends, and family members, to whom I owe more than I can ever repay.

I gratefully acknowledge the librarians and archivists who offered their vital assistance at many institutions, including the Schomburg Center for Research in Black Culture in New York City; the American Folklife Center at the Library of Congress, the Miami-Dade Public Library; the Manuscript Division of Princeton University Library; Special Collections, Florida Atlantic University Library, Boca Raton, Fla.; the Thomas G. Carpenter Library, University of North Florida, Jacksonville, Fla.; the Zora Neale Hurston Branch Library, Fort Pierce, Fla.; the Museum of Seminole County History, Sanford, Fla.; the Sanford Museum; the Ritz Theatre & LaVilla Museum, Jacksonville, Fla.; and the Jacksonville Public Library. I am particularly grateful to librarian Florence Turcotte and student assistant Tiffany Baglier of the Special and Area Studies Collections of the George A. Smathers Libraries at the University of Florida in Gainesville for their assistance with Hurston's "Herod the Great" manuscript.

I am most beholden to my husband Jay for his unwavering love, support, and encouragement; his scholarly knowledge and insights; and the financial and personal sacrifices he has cheerfully made. I am especially grateful to Jill "Jillyfish" Bowen, my sister, research assistant, and travel companion, for her stalwart confidence and constant encouragement. To Stetson Kennedy, who offered me his sage guidance as well as his peaceful Beluthahatchee home as a summer writing retreat, and to his wife Sandra Parks I offer my heartfelt thanks. I owe an enormous debt to Florida historian and friend David Nolan for his invaluable insights, support, and editorial advice and for pushing me along at just the right times. To my colleague Kim Grinder, who eagerly read and helped edit multiple versions of my manuscript, I offer my deepest gratitude. I am most appreciative to Bernard and Shirley Kinsey for their generous support.

My thanks go out to the staff of the University Press of Florida, particularly Acquisitions Director and Editor-in-Chief John Byram for his endless patience and to Director Meredith Morris-Babb for her encouragement and belief in the project. I also extend my gratitude to the generous individuals who granted me interviews: Sara Lee Creech, Patrick Duvall, Mildred Murrell, Bruce Smathers, Laura Helventon, Elizabeth Howard, Jean Parker Waterbury, Margaret A. Benton, Christina Maynor, Johnny Bullard, Helen Barr, Shirley Crawford, Marjorie Harrell, Ann Wilder, Camila Thompson, Weona Cleveland, Martha Huie, Sharon Hoffman, Carlton Jackson, Rosalie Gordon Mills, Margaret Paige, Art Johnson, Emily Zimmerman, Alan Lomax, and Stetson Kennedy.

Very special thanks to the community of Hurston scholars who offered their support and encouragement throughout the writing of this book: Deborah Plant, Pam Bordelon, Valerie Boyd, Gordon Patterson, Cheryl Wall, Carla Kaplan, Kristy Anderson, and Robert Hemenway. I am profoundly grateful for the generosity and invaluable guidance of John Lowe, who read and critiqued multiple copies of my manuscript and encouraged and challenged me to dig deeper. I also extend my thanks to the St. Lucie County Cultural Affairs Council and the Fort Pierce community for taking me in as one of their own and for honoring Hurston's legacy with its annual Zora Fest.

I offer my deepest thanks to the many friends, colleagues, and family members who inspired and encouraged me throughout this project and to those who read parts of my manuscript and offered valuable input; they include Kathy Ryan, Becky Davis, Gordon Poppell, Melody Conley, Terry Davis, Bobby Bowen, Tom Heller, Debra Craig, Holly Grossman, Mike Doyle, Anita Prentice, Patty Bates, Peggy Hand,

Melissa Dooley, Marcie Hagan, Darren Edgecomb, Manny Moya, Bob Carter, the late Bhetty Waldron, Susan Menke, Daryl Ross, Carrie Zimmerman, Carly Gates, Sheri Verge, Bob Fallon, Rosy Feliciano, Barb Grinder, Carole Koester, Mary Miller, Maria Lloyd, John Ward, Jodie Bonet, Adonnica Toler, Doretha Hair, Jack Connolly, Margaret Benton, Frank Roberts, Joe Garafolo, Becky Jones, Felicia Wilt, Danie Wilt, George Moylan, and the late Virginia Moylan. I am particularly grateful to Marie Pelfrey, Lynn Faller, and Sandy Aragon for their unfailing friendship and encouragement during the writing of this book.

To Dr. Lynne McGee, an inspiring educator, administrator, and literacy advocate, I offer my heartfelt gratitude for steering me to some vital research material that would have otherwise been overlooked. I would also like to thank Kate Babbitt for her infinite patience and superb editing skills.

My final thanks go to Alice Walker, who lifted Zora from the shadows and into the sunlight, and to Lucy Ann Hurston for keeping her "auntie's" legacy alive through her own talent, charm, and wit.

NOTES

Introduction

1. Alice Walker, *In Search of Our Mothers' Gardens* (San Diego: Harcourt, Brace, Jovanovich, 1983), 21.

Zora Neale Hurston: A Biographical Sketch, 1891–1948

Epigraph source: Zora Neale Hurston, *Dust Tracks on a Road* (1942; repr., New York: HarperPerennial, 1996), 1.

1. Kristy Anderson, "The Tangled Southern Roots of Zora Neale Hurston," typescript, in author's possession.

2. Hurston, *Dust Tracks*, 1.

3. Frank M. Otey, *Eatonville, Florida: A Brief History of One of America's First Freedman's Towns* (Winter Park, Fla.: Four-G Publishers, 1989), 6.

4. Altermese Smith Bentley, "Rev. John Hurston: 1900–1905," in *History of the First South Florida Missionary Baptist Association, 1888–1988* (Chuluota, Fla.: Mickler House, 1992), 111.

5. Otey, *Eatonville, Florida*, 11.

6. Booker T. Washington, *Up from Slavery* (1901), in *Three Negro Classics*, ed. John Hope Franklin (New York: Avon, 1965), 113.

7. Claudia Pierpont, "A Society of One," *The New Yorker*, February 17, 1997, 80.

8. Robert Hemenway, *Zora Neale Hurston, A Literary Biography* (Urbana: University of Illinois Press, 1977), 14.

9. Hurston, *Dust Tracks*, 46.

10. Ibid., 48.

11. Pamela Bordelon, ed., Go Gator *and* Muddy the Water: *Writings by Zora Neale Hurston from the Federal Writers' Project* (New York: W.W. Norton & Company, 1999), 76.

12. Hurston, *Dust Tracks*, 67.

13. Ibid., 98.

14. "Orange County Black Communities Survey," Phase 1, 28 September 1960, 76, Orange County Historical Society, Sanford Museum, Sanford, Florida.

15. Ibid.

16. R. L. Polk, *Sanford City Directory, 1909* (Columbus, Ohio: R. L. Polk & Company, 1909), 132. The house, which still stands today, is a large two-story empire-style house with three bedrooms and a spacious parlor.

17. Ibid.

18. "Orange County Black Communities Survey," 72.

19. Mildred Murrell, interview with author, Jacksonville, Florida, July 2001.

20. Ibid.

21. Hurston, *Dust Tracks*, 100.

22. Valerie Boyd, *Wrapped in Rainbows: The Life of Zora Neale Hurston* (New York: Scribner, 2003), 68.

23. Zora Neale Hurston, "How It Feels To Be Colored Me," *The World Tomorrow*, May 1928, 215–16.

24. Quoted in Boyd, *Wrapped in Rainbows*, 121.

25. Langston Hughes, "The New Negro Artist and the Racial Mountain," *The Nation*, June 23, 1926, 692–94.

26. Langston Hughes, *The Big Sea* (1940; repr., New York: Hill and Wang, 1993), 296.

27. Hurston, *Dust Tracks*, 144.

28. Boyd, *Wrapped in Rainbows*, 159.

29. Hurston, *Dust Tracks*, 150.

30. Ibid., 143–44.

31. Ibid., 150.

32. Ibid., 156.

33. ZNH to Langston Hughes, August 6, 1928, in *Zora Neale Hurston: A Life in Letters*, ed. Carla Kaplan (New York: Doubleday, 2002), 124.

34. ZNH to Franz Boas, April 21, 1929, in Kaplan, *Zora Neale Hurston*, 137.

35. Fannie Hurst, "Zora Neale Hurston: A Personality Sketch," *Yale University Library Gazette* 35 (July 1960): 20.

36. Boyd, *Wrapped in Rainbows*, 231.

37. Ibid., 257.

38. For a full discussion see Boyd, *Wrapped in Rainbows*, 258.

39. Hurston, *Dust Tracks*, 171.

40. Zora Neale Hurston, "Characteristics of Negro Expression," in Hurston, *The Sanctified Church*, ed. Toni Cade Bambara (Berkley, Ca: Turtle Island, 1983), 54.

41. Ibid.

42. Zora Neale Hurston, "Race Cannot Become Great Until It Recognizes Its Talent," *Washington Tribune*, December 29, 1934, 3.

43. Boyd, *Wrapped in Rainbows*, 268.

44. Ibid.

45. Ibid.

46. Ibid., 262.

47. Ibid., 285.

48. Ibid., 300.

49. For full discussion see Boyd, *Wrapped in Rainbows*, 300–306.

50. Ibid.

51. Bordelon, Go Gator *and* Muddy the Water, 16.

52. Johnnie Bullard, interview with author, White Springs, Florida, July 15, 2002.

53. Ibid.

54. Ibid.

55. Zora Neale Hurston to Albert Price, October 2, 1942, The Kinsey Collection: The Personal Treasures of Bernard & Shirley Kinsey, Norton Museum of Art, West Palm Beach, Florida.

56. Elizabeth Howard, telephone interview with author, June 12, 2006.

57. Ibid.

58. Ibid.

Chapter 1. In Hell's Basement

Epigraph Source: ZNH to Carl Van Vechten and Fania Marinoff, October 30, 1948, in *Zora Neale Hurston: A Life in Letters*, ed. Carla Kaplan (New York: Doubleday, 2002), 572, 574.

1. Ibid., 571.

2. Ibid., 572.

3. ZNH to Van Vechten, July 30, 1947, in Kaplan, *Zora Neale Hurston*, 551.

4. ZNH to Van Vechten and Fania Marinoff, October 30, 1948, in Kaplan, *Zora Neale Hurston*, 570.

5. Ibid., 572.

6. Ibid., 573.

7. Valerie Boyd, *Wrapped in Rainbows: The Life of Zora Neale Hurston* (New York: Scribner, 2003), 390.

8. Ibid., 391.

9. ZNH to Van Vechten, November 2, 1942, in Kaplan, *Zora Neale Hurston*, 466.

10. See Boyd, *Wrapped in Rainbows*, 391–92.

11. ZNH to Marjorie Kinnan Rawlings and Norton Baskin, December 22, 1948, in Kaplan, *Zora Neale Hurston*, 577.

12. Carla Kaplan, "'It Is Too Hard To Reveal One's Inner Self': The Forties," in Kaplan, *Zora Neale Hurston*, 435.

13. Ibid.

14. Boyd, *Wrapped in Rainbows*, 395.

15. Ibid.

16. ZNH to Van Vechten and Fania Marinoff, October 30, 1948, in Kaplan, *Zora Neale Hurston*, 573.

17. ZNH to Fannie Hurst, December 23, fall/winter 1948, in Kaplan, *Zora Neale Hurston*, 574.

18. Boyd, *Wrapped in Rainbows*, 398.

19. Kristy Anderson, "The Tangled Southern Roots of Zora Neale Hurston," typescript, in author's possession.

20. Ibid.

21. ZNH to William Clifford Hurston, May 2, 1949, in Kaplan, *Zora Neale Hurston*, 581.

22. Ibid.

Chapter 2. Sunshine and Southern Politics

Epigraph Source: Zora Neale Hurston, *Their Eyes Were Watching God*.(1942; repr., New York: HarperPerennial, 1996), 131.

1. ZNH to Burroughs Mitchell, January 24, 1950, in Carla Kaplan, ed., *Zora Neale Hurston: A Life in Letters* (New York: Doubleday, 2002), 624.

2. Ibid., 622.

3. Ibid., 621.

4. Ibid.

5. Ibid.

6. Helga H. Eason to Zora Neale Hurston, January 29, 1958, Miami-Dade County Public Library.

7. Valerie Boyd, *Wrapped in Rainbows: The Life of Zora Neale Hurston* (New York: Scribner, 2003), 363.

8. ZNH to Mitchell, January 24, 1950, in Kaplan, *Zora Neale Hurston*, 623.

9. Ibid.

10. Robert Hemenway, *Zora Neale Hurston: A Literary Biography* (Urbana: University of Illinois Press, 1977), 327.

11. James Lyons, "Famous Negro Author Working as Maid Here Just to 'Live a Little,'" *Miami Herald*, March 27, 1950.

12. ZNH to Burroughs Mitchell, March 1950, in Kaplan, *Zora Neale Hurston*, 627.

13. Sara Creech, interview with author, Lake Worth, Florida, June 2003.

14. *Miami Daily News*, April 5, 1944, quoted in James C. Clark, "Road to Defeat: Claude Pepper in the 1950 Florida Primary" (Ph.D. diss., University of Florida, 1998), 61.

15. *Florida Alligator*, December 17, 1948, quoted in Clark, "Road to Defeat," 62.

16. Campaign Memorandum, n.d., Claude Pepper Papers, Claude Pepper Center, Florida State University, Tallahassee, Florida.

17. Brian Lewis Crispell, *Testing the Limits: George Armistead Smathers and Cold War America* (Athens: University of Georgia Press, 1999), 61.

18. Ibid., 115.

19. Ibid., 59.

20. *Titusville Star-Advocate*, March 7, 1950, 2, quoted in Clark, "Road to Defeat," 64.

21. ZNH to Helen Worden Erskine, November 15, 1951, in Kaplan, *Zora Neale Hurston*, 680.

22. Ibid., 681.

23. Ibid.

24. Deborah Plant, *Every Tub Must Sit on Its Own Bottom: The Philosophy and Politics of Zora Neale Hurston* (Chicago: University of Illinois Press, 1996), 33.

25. Zora Neale Hurston, *Dust Tracks on a Road* (1942; repr., New York: HarperPerennial, 1996), 324–25.

26. Ben Green, *Before His Time: The Untold Story of Harry Moore, America's First Civil Rights Martyr* (New York: The Free Press, 1999), 117.

27. ZNH to Mitchell, July 21, 1950, in Kaplan, *Zora Neale Hurston*, 631.

28. Ibid.

29. ZNH to Mary Holland, June 27, 1957, in Kaplan, *Zora Neale Hurston*, 756.

30. Embassy of the Union of Soviet Socialist Republics, Information Bulletin, October 2, 1945, Claude Pepper Papers, Florida State University, quoted in Clark, "Road to Defeat," 78.

31. *New York Times*, October 1, 1945, quoted in Clark, "Road to Defeat," 78.

32. *Fort Lauderdale News*, September 21, 1945, quoted in Clark, "Road to Defeat," 79.

33. Clark, "Road To Defeat," 79.

34. *The Washington Post*, April 10, 1945, quoted in Clark, "Road to Defeat," 80.

35. Bruce Smathers, interview with author, Jacksonville, Florida, 2003.

36. Crispell, *Testing the Limits*, 66.

37. Ibid., 67.

38. *Miami Herald*, March 29, 1950, quoted in Clark, "Road to Defeat," 81.

39. Zora Neale Hurston, "I Saw Votes Peddled," *Negro Digest*, September 9, 1950.

40. Ibid.

41. Bill Baggs, "Were Negro Votes Bought In Miami?" *Herald News*, October 26, 1950.

42. Ibid.

Chapter 3. Sara Creech and Her Beautiful Doll

Epigraph source: Zora Neale Hurston to Sara Creech, June 29, 1950, in *Zora Neale Hurston: A Life in Letters*, ed. Carla Kaplan (New York: Doubleday, 2002), 629.

1. Sara Creech, interview with author, Lake Worth, Florida, July 2, 1994.

2. Ibid.

3. ZNH to Creech, June 29, 1950, in Kaplan, *Zora Neale Hurston*, 629.

4. "Negro Dolls for Christmas," *People Today*, December 5, 1950, 18.

5. "Modern Designs for Negro Dolls: Manufacturers Find Trends More Realistic," *Ebony*, January 1952, 46.

6. "Negro Dolls Popular with Public Since Birth in 1919," *Ebony*, January 1952, 46.

7. "Modern Designs for Negro Dolls," 46.

8. Ibid.

9. Ibid.

10. Richard Kluger, *Simple Justice* (New York: Random House, 1976), 318.

11. Zora Neale Hurston, *Dust Tracks on a Road* (1942; repr., New York: HarperPerennial, 1996), 185.

12. Ibid.

13. Zora Neale Hurston, *Their Eyes Were Watching God* (1937; repr., New York: HarperPerennial, 1998), 141.

14. Claudia Pierpont, "A Society of One," *The New Yorker*, February 19, 1999, 82.

15. Ibid.

16. Sara Creech, interview with author, Lake Worth, Florida, July 2, 1994.

17. Zora Neal Hurston to Sara Creech, June 29,1950, Creech Papers, in author's possession.

18. Ibid.

19. Sara Creech, interview with author, July 2, 1994.

20. Benjamin Mays to Sara Creech, November 9, 1950, Creech Papers, in author's possession.

21. ZNH to Mitchell, July 21, 1950, in Carla Kaplan, ed., *Zora Neale Hurston: A Life In Letters* (New York: Doubleday, 2002), 630.

22. ZNH to Jean Parker Waterbury, March 6, 1951, in Kaplan, *Zora Neale Hurston*, 647.

23. ZNH to Mitchell, July 21, 1950, in Kaplan, *Zora Neale Hurston*, 631.

24. Valerie Boyd, *Wrapped in Rainbows: The Life of Zora Neale Hurston* (New York: Scribner, 2003), 407.

25. Sara Creech, interview with author, Lake Worth, Florida, July 3,1994.

26. Ibid.

27. ZNH to Maxeda von Hesse, April 7, 1951, in Kaplan, *Zora Neale Hurston*, 650–52.

28. Sara Creech, interview with author, July 3, 1994.

29. ZNH to Waterbury, February 2, 1951, in Kaplan, *Zora Neale Hurston*, 638.

30. Robert Hemenway, *Zora Neale Hurston: A Literary Biography* (1977; repr., Urbana: University of Illinois Press, 1980), 340.

31. ZNH to Waterbury, May 1, 1951, in Kaplan, *Zora Neale Hurston*, 655–56.

32. Ibid., 656.

33. Hemenway, *Zora Neale Hurston*, 307.

34. Zora Neale Hurston, "What White Publishers Won't Print," *Negro Digest*, April 1950, 85–89.

35. Burroughs Mitchell to Zora Neale Hurston, October 3, 1950, Archives of Charles Scribner's Sons, Department of Rare Books and Special Collections, Princeton University Library, Princeton, New Jersey.

36. Boyd, *Wrapped in Rainbows*, 408.

37. ZNH to Charles S. Johnson, December 5, 1950, in Kaplan, *Zora Neale Hurston*, 633.

38. Ibid., 634.

39. Sara Creech, interview with author, West Palm Beach, Florida, August 17, 1995.

40. Ibid.

41. Ibid.

42. Hurston, *Their Eyes*, 131.

43. Sara Creech, interview with author, West Palm Beach, Florida, August 7, 1995.

44. Christine Maynor, telephone interview with author, June 13, 2004.

45. Ibid.

46. Sara Creech, interview with author, August 8, 1995, Lake Worth, Florida.

47. ZNH to Carl Sandberg, February 13, 1951, in Kaplan, *Zora Neale Hurston*, 641.

48. Sara Creech, interview with author, Lake Worth, Florida, July 14, 1995.

49. Ibid.

50. ZNH to Sandberg, February 13, 1951, in Kaplan, *Zora Neale Hurston*, 641.

51. Sara Creech, interview with author, Lake Worth, Florida, July 20, 1995.

52. Ibid.

53. Ibid.

54. Ibid.

55. Ibid.

56. Carla Kaplan, "'Being "Different" Has Its Drawbacks': The Fifties," in Kaplan, *Zora Neale Hurston*, 613.

57. Ibid.

58. Ibid.

59. Ibid.

60. Alec Wilkinson, *Big Sugar* (New York: Alfred A. Knopf, 1989), 4.

61. Ibid., 6.

62. Ibid.

63. ZNH to Waterbury, March 6, 1951, in Kaplan, *Zora Neale Hurston*, 647.

64. Sara Creech, Maxeda von Hesse, and Sheila Burlingame, "The History of How the Sara Lee Doll Came to Be," 3, typescript, Creech Papers, in author's possession.

65. Ibid.

66. "Guest List for Mrs. Roosevelt's Tea," typescript, Creech Papers, in author's possession.

67. ZNH to Waterbury, March 18, 1951, in Kaplan, *Zora Neale Hurston*, 650.

68. Sara Creech, interview with author, Lake Worth, Florida, August 28, 1994.

69. ZNH to von Hesse, April 7, 1951, in Kaplan, *Zora Neale Hurston*, 651.

70. ZNH to Waterbury, April 9,1951, in Kaplan, *Zora Neale Hurston*, 653.

71. ZNH to Waterbury, May 10,1951, in Kaplan, *Zora Neale Hurston*, 657.

72. Jean Parker Waterbury, telephone interview with author, May 5, 2000.

73. Ibid.

Chapter 4. Herod the Sun-Like Splendor

Epigraph source: Zora Neale Hurston, "Herod the Great," ms., "Preface A," 2, Zora Neale Hurston Papers, Special and Area Studies Collections, George A. Smathers Libraries, University of Florida, Gainesville.

1. Zora Neale Hurston to Burroughs Mitchell, July 15, 1951, in Carla Kaplan, ed., *Zora Neale Hurston: A Life In Letters* (New York: Doubleday, 2002), 667.

2. Karen Raley and Ann Raley Flotte, *Melbourne and Eau Gallie* (Chicago: Arcadia Publishing, 2002), 14.

3. ZNH to Jean Parker Waterbury, July 9, 1951, in Kaplan, *Zora Neale Hurston*, 663.

4. Sara Creech, interview with author, Lake Worth, Florida, August 28, 1994.

5. ZNH to Waterbury, August 8, 1951, in Kaplan, *Zora Neale Hurston*, 673.

6. ZNH to Mitchell, July 15, 1951, in Kaplan, *Zora Neale Hurston*, 670.

7. Ibid.

8. ZNH to Waterbury, July 9, 1951, in Kaplan, *Zora Neale Hurston*, 663–64.

9. ZNH to Mitchell, July 15, 1951, in Kaplan, *Zora Neale Hurston*, 668.

10. Lora S. Britt, "Zora Neale Hurston—Novelist, Folklorist, Anthropologist," *The River Valley Funlander*, March 3, 1978.

11. Ibid.

12. Ibid.

13. Ibid.

14. Ibid.

15. Ibid.

16. Ibid.

17. Ibid.

18. ZNH to Waterbury, August 8, 1951, in Kaplan, *Zora Neale Hurston*, 674.

19. ZNH to Carl Van Vechten, September 12, 1945, in Kaplan, *Zora Neale Hurston*, 530.

20. Ibid., 529.

21. Ibid., 530.

22. Ibid., 531.

23. Ibid.

24. Ibid., 532.

25. ZNH to Mary Holland, June 13, 1955, in Kaplan, *Zora Neale Hurston*, 730.

26. ZNH to Mitchell, July/August 1951, in Kaplan, *Zora Neale Hurston*, 665.

27. ZNH to Mary Holland, June 13, 1955, in Kaplan, *Zora Neale Hurston*, 732.

28. ZNH to Waterbury, July 9, 1951, in Kaplan, *Zora Neale Hurston*, 664.

29. ZNH to Mitchell, October 2, 1953, in Kaplan, *Zora Neale Hurston*, 702.

30. Robert Green, *Herod the Great* (New York: Franklin Watts, 1996), 7.

31. Stewart Perowne, *The Life and Times of Herod the Great* (London: Camelot Press, 1956), 176.

32. Peter Richardson, *Herod: King of the Jews and Friend of the Romans* (Minneapolis: Fortress Press, 1990), 3.

33. Green, *Herod the Great*, 37.

34. Ibid., 9.

35. Zora Neale Hurston, *Dust Tracks on a Road* (1942; repr., New York: HarperPerennial, 1996), 254–55.

36. ZNH to Mitchell, October 2, 1953, in Kaplan, *Zora Neale Hurston*, 703.

37. Deborah Plant, *Zora Neale Hurston: A Biography of the Spirit* (Westport, Conn.: Praeger, 2007), 138.

38. Carla Kaplan, in Kaplan, *Zora Neale Hurston*, 604.

39. Plant, *Zora Neale Hurston*, 143.

40. Perowne, *Herod the Great*, 16.

41. Plant, *Zora Neale Hurston*, 143.

42. See Perowne, *The Life and Times of Herod the Great*; and Richardson, *Herod: King of the Jews and Friend of the Romans*.

43. Hurston, "Herod the Great," "Preface A," 8.

44. ZNH to Waterbury, July 15, 1951, in Kaplan, *Zora Neale Hurston*, 730.

45. Hurston, "Herod the Great," Volume I, "Introduction B," 10.

46. Ibid., 3.

47. Ibid.

48. Hurston, "Herod the Great," Volume I, "Introduction A," 2.

49. Hurston, "Herod the Great," "Preface A," 5.

50. Ibid., 1.

51. Ibid., 6.

52. Hurston, "Herod the Great," "Introduction A," 2.

53. ZNH to Waterbury, July 15, 1951, in Kaplan, *Zora Neale Hurston*, 732.

54. Ibid., 730.

55. Green, *Herod the Great*, 12–13.

56. Ibid., 15.

57. Ibid.

58. Hurston, "Herod the Great," Volume I, "Introduction A, 2.

59. Ibid.

60. Ibid.

61. Ibid.

62. Ibid., 30.

63. Hurston, "Herod the Great," Volume III, 55–56.

64. Ibid., 69.

65. Ibid., 74.

66. Ibid., 104.

67. Hurston, "Herod the Great," Volume V, 243.

68. Plant, *Zora Neale Hurston*, 147.

69. Hurston, "Herod the Great," Volume V, 32.

70. Ibid., 163.

71. Ibid., 42.

72. Ibid., 205.

73. Green, *Herod the Great*, 39.

74. ZNH to Mitchell, July/August 1951, in Kaplan, *Zora Neale Hurston*, 665.

75. Valerie Boyd, *Wrapped in Rainbows: The Life of Zora Neale Hurston* (New York: Scribner, 2003), 212.

76. Robert Hemenway, *Zora Neale Hurston: A Literary Biography* (1977; repr., Urbana: University of Illinois Press, 1980), 341.

77. ZNH to Edward Everette Hurston, October 12, 1951, in Kaplan, *Zora Neale Hurston*, 677.

78. ZNH to Waterbury, March 6, 1952, in Kaplan, *Zora Neale Hurston*, 683.

79. ZNH to Mitchell, May 1, 1952, in Kaplan, *Zora Neale Hurston*, 685.

Chapter 5. Death on the Suwannee

Epigraph source: ZNH to William Bradford Huie, June 10, 1954, in *Zora Neale Hurston: A Life in Letters*, ed. Carla Kaplan (New York: Doubleday, 2002), 713, 715.

1. ZNH to Huie, May 14, 1954, in Kaplan, *Zora Neale Hurston*, 710.

2. Zora Neale Hurston, "The Life Story of Mrs. Ruby J. McCollum!" (Installment 1), *Pittsburgh Courier*, February 28, 1953.

3. William Bradford Huie, *Ruby McCollum: Woman in the Suwannee Jail* (New York: Dutton, 1956), 24–25.

4. Ibid., 25–26.

5. Ibid.

6. Laura Helventon, telephone interview with author, July 20, 2001.

7. Huie, *Ruby McCollum*, 28.

8. Ibid., 55.

9. Ben Green, *Before His Time: The Untold Story of Harry T. Moore, America's First Civil Rights Martyr* (New York: The Free Press, 1999), 137.

10. Huie, *Ruby McCollum*, 53.

11. Zora Neale Hurston, "Zora's Revealing Story of Ruby's 1st Day in Court," *Pittsburgh Courier*, October 11, 1952.

12. Ibid., 14.

13. Huie, *Ruby McCollum*, 95.

14. Ibid., 14.

15. Hurston, "Zora's Revealing Story."

16. Ibid.

17. Ibid.

18. Ibid.

19. Zora Neale Hurston, "The Life Story of Mrs. Ruby J. McCollum!" (Installment 4), *Pittsburgh Courier*, March 21, 1953.

20. Zora Neale Hurston, "The Life Story of Mrs. Ruby J. McCollum!" (Installment 5), *Pittsburgh Courier*, March 28, 1953.

21. Ibid.

22. Carlton Jackson, telephone interview with author, July 12, 2001.

23. Hurston, "The Life Story of Mrs. Ruby J. McCollum!" (Installment 5).

24. Ibid.

25. Ibid.

26. Ibid.

27. Zora Neale Hurston, "My Impressions of the Trial," in Huie, *Ruby McCollum*, 91.

28. ZNH to Huie, May 14, 1954, in Kaplan, *Zora Neale Hurston*, 709.

29. Ibid., 710.

30. Hurston, "My Impressions of the Trial," in Huie, *Ruby McCollum*, 98.

31. Ibid., 89.

32. Quoted in ibid., 100.

33. Ibid., 101.

34. Huie, *Ruby McCollum*, 8.

35. ZNH to Huie, March 28, 1954, in Kaplan, *Zora Neale Hurston*, 705.

36. Huie, *Ruby McCollum*, 48.

37. Ibid., 153.

38. Ibid., 154.

39. Ibid.

40. Ibid., 111.

41. Ibid., 113.

42. Ibid.

43. ZNH to Huie, June 10, 1954, in Kaplan, *Zora Neale Hurston*, 712.

Chapter 6. A Crisis in Dixie

Epigraph source: Zora Neale Hurston, "Court Order Can't Make Races Mix," *Orlando Sentinel*, August 11, 1955.

1. ZNH to Herbert Sheen, March 4, 1953, in *Zora Neale Hurston: A Life in Letters*, ed. Carla Kaplan (New York: Doubleday, 2002), 690.

2. Ibid., 691.

3. Ibid., 692.

4. Ibid., 693.

5. Quoted in Valerie Boyd, *Wrapped in Rainbows: The Life of Zora Neale Hurston* (New York: Scribner, 2003), 351.

6. Ibid.

7. ZNH to Marjorie Kinnan Rawlings, May 16, 1943, in Kaplan, *Zora Neale Hurston*, 486.

8. ZNH to Carl Van Vechten, July 30, 1947, in Kaplan, *Zora Neale Hurston*, 551.

9. ZNH to Mary Holland, June 13, 1955, in Kaplan, *Zora Neale Hurston*, 728.

10. Ibid.

11. Quoted in Boyd, *Wrapped in Rainbows*, 423.

12. Robert Hemenway, *Zora Neale Hurston: A Literary Biography* (1977; repr., Urbana: University of Illinois Press, 1980), 345.

13. ZNH to Burroughs Mitchell, August 12, 1955, in Kaplan, *Zora Neale Hurston*, 741.

14. Ibid.

15. Quoted in Boyd, *Wrapped in Rainbows*, 427.

16. Zora Neale Hurston, "The Enemy: A Unique Personal Experience" (1955), 1, Zora Neale Hurston Papers, Special and Area Studies Collections, George A. Smathers Libraries, University of Florida, Gainesville.

17. Ibid., 2.

18. Ibid., 1.

19. Ibid., 2.

20. Ibid., 3.

21. Ibid.

22. Ibid., 1.

23. Ibid.

24. Ibid., 4.

25. Ibid.

26. Ibid., 6.

27. Ibid.

28. Ibid.

29. Ibid., 7.

30. Ibid.

31. Ibid.

32. Ibid.

33. Lynn Moylan, "A Child Cannot Be Taught By Anyone Who Despises Him," in *The Inside Light: New Critical Essays on Zora Neale Hurston*, ed. Deborah G. Plant (Westport, Conn.: Praeger Publishers, 2010), 216.

34. Ibid.

35. Ibid.

36. Hurston, "Court Order Can't Make Races Mix."

37. Ibid.

38. Edward D. Davis, *A Half Century of Struggle for Freedom in Florida* (Orlando: Drake's Publishing, 1981), 131.

39. Harry S. Ashmore, *The Negro and the Schools* (Chapel Hill: University of North Carolina Press, 1954), 153.

40. Davis, *A Half Century of Struggle for Freedom*, 131.

41. Ashmore, *The Negro and the Schools*, 156.

42. Ibid., 153.

43. Ibid., 152.

44. Ibid., 155.

45. Asa G. Hilliard, III, "Foreword," in Vivian Gunn Morris and Curtis L. Morris, *The Price They Paid: Desegregation in an African American Community* (New York: Teachers College Press, 2002), x.

46. Hemenway, *Zora Neale Hurston*, 336.

47. Quoted in Deborah Plant, *Every Tub Must Sit on Its Own Bottom: The Philosophy and Politics of Zora Neale Hurston* (Chicago: University of Illinois Press, 1996), 117.

48. Morris and Morris, *The Price They Paid*, 3.

49. Hilliard, "Foreword," xi.

50. Quoted in Samuel G. Freedman, "Still Separate, Still Unequal," *New York Times*, May 16, 2004.

51. Brian J. Daugherity and Charles C. Bolton, ed., *With All Deliberate Speed: Implementing Brown v. Board of Education* (Fayetteville: University of Arkansas Press, 2008), 142.

52. C.[harles] V. Hamilton, "Race and Education: A Search for Legitimacy," *Harvard Educational Review* 38, no. 4 (1968): 669–84.

53. Moylan, "A Child Cannot Be Taught By Anyone Who Despises Him," 219.

54. John Bartlow Martin, *The Deep South Says Never* (New York: Ballantine Books, 1957), 11.

55. Ibid., 12.

56. Ibid., 11.

57. Moylan, "A Child Cannot Be Taught By Anyone Who Despises Him," 220.

58. ZNH to Margrit De Sablonière, in Kaplan, *Zora Neale Hurston*, 747.

59. Morris and Morris, *The Price They Paid*, 78.

60. Derrick Bell, *Silent Covenants: Brown v. Board of Education and the Unfulfilled Hopes for Racial Reform* (New York: Oxford University Press, 2004), 112.

61. Moylan, "A Child Cannot Be Taught By Anyone Who Despises Him," 220.

62. Bell, *Silent Covenants*, 96–97.

63. Moylan, "A Child Cannot Be Taught By Anyone Who Despises Him," 221.

64. Ibid.

65. Ibid.

66. Ibid., 218.

67. Sara Lee Creech, interview with author, Lake Worth, Florida, August 3, 1994.

68. Ibid.

69. Quoted in Elizabeth Sutton, "A Visit with Zora Neale Hurston," typescript, July 1956, in author's possession.

70. Quoted in ibid.

71. Quoted in ibid.

72. Quoted in ibid.

73. Boyd, *Wrapped in Rainbows*, 425.

Chapter 7. The Last Horizon

1. Zora Neale Hurston, *Dust Tracks on a Road* (1942; repr., New York: HarperPerennial, 1996), 365.

2. Quoted in John Hicks, "Discovery," in *Zora! Zora Neale Hurston: A Woman and Her Community*, ed. N. Y. Nathiri (Orlando: Sentinel Communications, 1991), 37.

3. ZNH to Mary Holland, July 2, 1957, in *Zora Neale Hurston: A Life in Letters*, ed. Carla Kaplan (New York: Doubleday, 2002), 761.

4. ZNH to Holland, June 27, 1957, in Kaplan, *Zora Neale Hurston*, 759.

5. Ibid.

6. Ibid.

7. ZNH to Holland, July 2, 1957, in Kaplan, *Zora Neale Hurston*, 761.

8. Spessard L. Holland, interview with Bill Henry, recorded for the WFLA-TV program *The Holland Years*, ca. 1971, archived at Special and Area Studies Collections, George A. Smathers Libraries, University of Florida, Gainesville.

9. Ibid.

10. Ibid.

11. ZNH to Holland, July 2, 1957, in Kaplan, *Zora Neale Hurston*, 763.

12. Ibid., 764.

13. ZNH to Holland, June 27, 1957, in Kaplan, *Zora Neale Hurston*, 756.

14. Ibid., 757.

15. ZNH to Herbert Sheen, June 28, 1957, in Kaplan, *Zora Neale Hurston*, 755.

16. Ibid.

17. Hicks, "Discovery," 41.

18. Helen Barr, telephone interview with author, July 3, 2006.

19. Art Johnson, telephone interview with author, May 23, 2006.

20. Hicks, "Discovery," 39.

21. Ibid.

22. Ibid., 40.

23. Margaret Benton, interview with author, Fort Pierce, Florida, July 20, 2004.

24. Shirley Crawford, telephone interview with author, July 6, 2004.

25. Marjorie Harrell, interview with author, Fort Pierce, Florida, July 10, 2004.

26. Ibid.

27. Cleo Leathe, telephone interview with author, July 6, 2004.

28. ZNH to Mitchell Ferguson, March 7, 1958, in Kaplan, *Zora Neale Hurston*, 768.

29. Ibid., 767.

30. Ibid., 766.

31. Ibid., 767.

32. Gordon Patterson, "Zora Neale Hurston as English Teacher: A Lost Chapter Found," *The Marjorie Kinnan Rawlings Journal of Florida Literature* 5 (1993): 57.

33. George Beebe to Doug Silver, July 9, 1958, Miami-Dade Public Library.

34. Zora Neale Hurston to Sara Creech, October 20, 1958, Creech Papers, in author's possession.

35. Ibid.

36. Hicks, "Discovery," 42.

37. Ibid.

38. ZNH to Harper Brothers Publishers, January 16, 1959, in Kaplan, *Zora Neale Hurston*, 771.

39. Ann Wilder, interview with author, Port St. Lucie, Florida, July 6, 2003.

40. Ibid.

41. "Final Rites Sunday for Author Zora Neale Hurston at Peeks," *The Chronicle*, February 12, 1960, 11.

42. Ann Wilder, interview with author, July 6, 2003.

43. Rev. W. A. Jennings, Sr., quoted in Theodore Pratt, "Zora Neale Hurston," *Florida Quarterly* 40 (July 1961).

44. Pratt, "Zora Neale Hurston," 35.

45. Carl Van Vechten to Harold Jackman, February 10, 1960, Countee Cullen Memorial Collection, Arnett Library, Atlanta University, Atlanta, Georgia.

46. Quoted in Boyd, *Wrapped in Rainbows*, 435.

47. Patrick Duval, interview with author, Fort Pierce, Florida, July 10, 2001.

Conclusion

1. Zora Neale Hurston, *Dust Tracks on a Road* (1942; repr., New York: HarperPerennial, 1996), 14.

2. ZNH to William Bradford Huie, May 14, 1954, in *Zora Neale Hurston: A Life in Letters*, ed. Carla Kaplan (New York: Doubleday, 2002), 709.

3. Zora Neale Hurston, "Crazy for This Democracy," *Negro Digest*, April 1945, 37.

4. John Lowe, *Jump at the Sun: Zora Neale Hurston's Cosmic Comedy* (Chicago: University of Illinois Press, 1994), 3.

5. Stewart Perowne, *The Life and Times of Herod the Great* (London: Camelot Press, 1956), 4; and Peter Richardson, *Herod: King of the Jews and Friend of the Romans* (Minneapolis: Fortress Press, 1990), 7.

6. Lowe, *Jump at the Sun*, 2.

7. Hurston, *Dust Tracks on a Road*, 231.

8. Ibid., 268.

SELECT BIBLIOGRAPHY

Ashmore, Harry S. *The Negro and the Schools*. Chapel Hill: The University of North Carolina Press, 1954.

Bell, Derrick. *Silent Covenants: Brown v. Board of Education and the Unfulfilled Hopes for Racial Reform*. Oxford: Oxford University Press, 2004.

Boyd, Valerie. *Wrapped in Rainbows: The Life of Zora Neale Hurston*. New York: Scribner, 2003.

Britt, Lora S. "Zora Neale Hurston—Novelist, Folklorist, Anthropologist." *The River Valley Funlander*, March 3, 1978.

Caldas, Stephen J., and Carl L. Bankston, III. *Forced to Fail*. Westport: Praeger, 2005.

Clark, James C. "Road to Defeat: Claude Pepper in the 1950 Florida Primary." Ph.D. diss., University of Florida, 1998.

Crispell, Brian Lewis. *Testing the Limits: George Armistead Smathers and Cold War America*. Athens: University of Georgia Press, 1999.

Daugherity, Brian J., and Charles C. Bolton, eds. *With All Deliberate Speed: Implementing Brown v. Board of Education*. Fayetteville: University of Arkansas Press, 2008.

Davis, Edward D. *A Half Century of Struggle for Freedom In Florida*, Orlando: Drake's Publishing, 1981.

Green, Ben. *Before His Time: The Untold Story of Harry Moore, America's First Civil Rights Martyr*. New York: The Free Press, 1999.

Green, Robert. *Herod the Great*. New York: Franklin Watts, 1996.

Hemenway, Robert. *Zora Neal Hurston: A Literary Biography*. Urbana: University of Illinois Press, 1977.

Hughes, Langston. "The New Negro Artist and the Racial Mountain." *The Nation*, June 23, 1926, 692–94.

———. *The Big Sea*. 1940; repr., New York: Hill and Wang, 1993.

Huie, William Bradford. *Ruby McCollum: Woman in the Suwannee Jail*. New York: Dutton, 1956.

Hurst, Fannie. "Zora Neale Hurston: A Personality Sketch." *Yale University Library Gazette*, July 1960, 20.

Hurston, Zora Neale. "Characteristics of Negro Expression." In Hurston, *The Sancti-fied Church*, ed. Toni Cade Bambara. 1934; repr., Berkley, Calif.: Turtle Island, 1983.

———. "Court Order Can't Make Races Mix." *Orlando Sentinel*, August 11, 1955.

———. *Dust Tracks on a Road*. 1942; repr., New York: HarperPerennial, 1996.

———. "How It Feels to Be Colored Me." *The World Tomorrow*, May 1928.

———. "I Saw Votes Peddled." *Negro Digest*, September 9, 1950.

———. "Race Cannot Become Great Until It Recognizes Its Talent." *Washington Tri-bune*, December 29, 1934, 3.

———. *Their Eyes Were Watching God*. 1942; repr., New York: HarperPerennial, 1996.

———. "The Life of Ruby McCollum!" Installment 4. *Pittsburgh Courier*, March 21, 1953.

———. "The Life of Ruby McCollum!" Installment 5. *Pittsburgh Courier*, March 28, 1953.

———. "Zora's Revealing Story of Ruby's 1st Day in Court." *Pittsburgh Courier*, October 11, 1952.

Kaplan, Carla, ed. *Zora Neale Hurston: A Life in Letters*. New York: Doubleday, 2002.

Lyons, James. "Famous Negro Author Working as Maid Here Just to 'Live a Little.'" *Miami Herald*, March 27, 1950.

Martin, John Bartlow. *The Deep South Says Never*. New York: Ballantine Books, 1957.

"Modern Designs for Negro Dolls: Manufacturers Find Trends More Realistic." *Ebony*, January 1952, 46.

Morris, Vivian Gunn, and Curtis L. Morris. *The Price They Paid: Desegregation in an African American Community*. New York: Teacher's College Press, 2002.

"Negro Dolls for Christmas." *People Today*, December 5, 1950.

"Negro Dolls Popular with Public since Birth in 1919." *Ebony*, January 1952, 46.

Otey, Frank. *Eatonville, Florida: A Brief History of One of America's First Freedman's Towns*. Winter Park, Fla.: Four-G Publishers, 1989.

Patterson, Gordon. "Zora Neale Hurston as English Teacher: A Lost Chapter Found." *The Marjorie Kinnan Rawlings Journal of Florida Literature* 5 (1993): 57.

Perowne, Stewart. *The Life and Times of Herod the Great*. London: Camelot Press, 1956.

Pierpont, Claudia. "A Society of One." *The New Yorker*, February 17, 1997, 80–82.

Plant, Deborah G. *A Biography of the Spirit: Zora Neale Hurston*. Westport, Conn.: Praeger, 2007.

———. *Every Tub Must Sit on Its Own Bottom: The Philosophy and Politics of Zora Neale Hurston*. Chicago: University of Illinois Press, 1995.

———, ed. *The Inside Light: New Essays on Zora Neale Hurston*. Westport, Conn.: Praeger, 2010.

Pratt, Theodore. "Zora Neale Hurston." *Florida Quarterly* 40 (July 1961): 35–40.

Raley, Karen, and Ann Raley Flotte. *Melbourne and Eau Gallie*. Chicago: Arcadia Publishing, 2002.

Richardson, Peter. *Herod: King of the Jews and Friend of the Romans*. Minneapolis: Fortress Press, 1999.

Washington, Booker T. *Up from Slavery*. (1901). In *Three Negro Classics*, ed. John Hope Franklin. New York: Avon, 1965.

Wilkinson, Alec. *Big Sugar*. New York: Alfred A. Knopf, 1989.

INDEX

Virginia Lynn Moylan is an independent scholar and founding member of the Fort Pierce, Florida, Annual Zora Festival. She has taught English and literature in Palm Beach County for twenty-one years and is a contributing author to *The Inside Light: New Critical Essays on Zora Neale Hurston* (Praeger Publishers, 2010).